An Plywyow a Gernow - The Parishes

Much has been written about place-n_____
last few centuries. Maybe this is _____
culture is bound up in them and it .. ... ~~... ....
makes it an honour to live in Cornwall.

The Religious Communities of Cornwall

According to Lynette Olson, the monastic movement reached Britain around 500 AD. Monasteries were set up at St. Buryan, St. Keverne, St. Piran's Oratory, Crantock, Probus, Padstow, Golant, St. Neot, St. Kew, Looe Island and St. Germans. They were founded in the name of **Beryan, Aghevran, Pyran, Karentek, Proboes, Gwedhenek, Samson, Niet, Dogho** and possibly an unknown saint by the name of **Aled**. Through the course of history they became parishes.

The greatest single event that created the largest number of Cornish religious communities (and hence parishes being founded) was the invasion of the Kingdom of Brechan in Wales by the Irish war-lord Analgaidh in or around 530 AD. Cornish legend says that King Brechan had no fewer than twenty four children and fifteen of them went on to start religious communities in Cornwall. These then evolved into the familiar parishes of Advent, Egloskerry, Endellion, Gwennap, Landulph, Lanteglos by Camelford, Mevagissey, Morwenstow, St. Issey, St. Juliot, St. Keyne, St. Mabyn, St. Minver, St. Teath and St. Wenn.

Kingdoms of the Celts by John King tells us that Saint David converted the people of what is now Wales to Christianity around 550 AD. Not only is the patron saint of Wales honoured in the parish of Davidstow but his mother **Nonna** is also commemorated by having the parish of Altarnun named after her. Other saints from Wales include **Sen Samson** born in Wales and venerated at Golant and Southhill and went on to be one of the founding fathers of the Breton church. **Ke, Fili** and **Kubert** also came to Cornwall from Wales, established religious communities and gave their names to Cornish parishes.

Saints **Briek, Budhek, Day, Meryasek, Mewan, Ostell**, and many others crossed the sea from Brittany. They performed miracles, founded communities and left Cornwall a great legacy of parishes founded by Breton saints; St. Brioc, Budock, St. Day, Camborne, St. Mewan and St. Austell.

As well as Wales and Brittany many Irish saints founded Cornish parishes. Many of these are centred around St. Ives Bay where, legend has it that, a great storm blew a ship of Irish pilgrims onto the sands. The local king thought he was being invaded and killed most of them but **Gwynnyer, Goedhyan, Erk, Ia** and others escaped to form the parishes now known to us as Gwinear, Gwithian, St. Erth and St. Ives.

The greatest Cornish saint is also from Ireland. **Pyran** landed at Perranporth in what is now the parish of Perranzabuloe. However there are two other parishes, Perranarworthal and Perranuthnoe, that bear his name. **Pyran** is the patron saint of tinners and one of the three patron saints of Cornwall together with Saint Petroc and Saint Michael. It is the white cross of **Pyran** on a black ground that is flown as the national flag of Cornwall.

The ancient parishes of Cornwall were long established when King Athelstan of Wessex ethnically cleansed Exeter and then Devon of Celtic people in 936 and set the border as the River Tamar. The diocese of Cornwall was dissolved, and absorbed into that of Crediton in Devon c.1040. The parishes developed and continued through the establishment of Cornwall as an earldom in the Norman Empire and then as a duchy after 1337. Although the established church was Catholic up to 1549, the ancient parishes continued into the nineteenth century.

It is at this point that many new parishes were created in order to accommodate the shifting settlement patterns of Cornwall's population. No fewer than forty-five new parishes were created in the eighteen hundreds. Undoubtedly some were formed to accommodate the rapid population increase in the mining districts. See parishes with dates in the main table below.

The modern parishes of Penzance are St. Mary, founded in 1791, St. Paul in 1867 and St. John in 1881. In Truro, the ancient parish of St. Mary was joined by the modern parishes of St. George in 1847, St. John in 1852 and St. Paul 1865. Sadly there is no Saint Ringo!

In the Cornwall of today, with mass car ownership, many parishes are not so much centres of worship as focal points of community.

Cornish Forms

Throughout history there have been Cornish speaking communities and from 1300, English speaking communities living in Cornwall. Therefore we find many places with a Cornish name and an English name for the same place. St. Ives was *Seint Ive* 1346, *Seint Ithe* 1347, *Sent Ia* 1468 and *St. Ies* but also *Porthye* 1284, *Porthia* 1291 and *Poreeah* c.1670. This bilingualism existed right across the country; St. Germans, in the south eastern corner, was *Sanctus Germanus* 994 and *Lannaledensis* c. 950. St. Teath, in North Cornwall, was *Sancta Tetha* c.1190 and *Egglostetha* c. 1190. Probus, in Mid Cornwall, was *Seynt Probus* 1466 and *Lamprobus* 1759. St. Just in Penwith, in the far west, was *Yust* 1524 and *Lanuste* 1396.

The Cornish scholar and historian Charles Henderson wrote the largest part of *The Cornish Church Guide*, published in 1925. What is notable about this book is the list of churches in Cornwall. Henderson states the dedication and the Cornish form. Thus we find, "Minster. D. *St. Merteriana Virgin.* C. *Talkarn*, St. Kea. D. *St. Keus* or *Ke.* C. *Landegea*, St. Ives. D. *St. Ia Virgin.* C. *Porthia.*" etc. As these Cornish forms relate to the Churches of Cornwall they also often related to the parishes. As well as Cornish forms Henderson even differentiates between English and Cornish spelling, e.g. "Treslothan. D. *St. John.* C. *Tresulwethen.*" Treslothan is derived from **tre** 'farm, settlement' + **Sulwethan** 'a British personal name' and the parish created out of Camborne in 1845.

The renowned scholar of Cornish topography, Dr. Oliver Padel, uses parishes to identify particular place-names. Also the Place-name Working Group of **Kesva an Taves Kernewek,** (the Cornish Language Board) holds seminars and publishes in the medium of Cornish. So a definitive list of parish names with their Cornish language forms is now needed. Indeed plotting various place-name information on a parish by parish level provides sufficient accuracy for conclusions to be drawn for Cornwall as a whole.

Cornish Parishes and their Cornish Language Forms

The dates that occasionally appear in the first column are of their first registers. All parishes without a date are considered 'ancient.'

The second column contains the Cornish name of the parish not the settlement that may be of the same name, thus, **Heyl Sen Elwyn** is the Cornish form of the parish and **Heyl** simply the Cornish form of the town.

The third column contains a code, the key to which is listed below.

Code Letter	Meaning
K	an element which is attested, understood and respelled as necessary
M	an obscure element, re-spelled according to examples from Middle Cornish and the principles of Kernewek Kemmyn
N	a new translation of a non-Cornish element
H	a Celtic personal name
P	a non-Celtic personal name
S	an obscure (sometimes) element, or elements, rendered in Kernewek Kemmyn according to sound rather than meaning
A	an additional element

The fourth column contains historic forms that support the Cornish forms in the second column. Approximate English meanings are given in single speech marks.

English	Cornish	Code	Approximate English meaning and supporting historic form(s)
Advent	Sen Adhwynn	NH	'Saint Adhwynn' *Seint Athwane* 1435, *Adven* 1349
St. Agnes	Breanek	KM	'Hill + obscure element' *Bryanick* 1884
St. Agnes (Scilly)	Pennpras	NN	'head, end of the pasture' *Hagenesse* 1194 < Norse *hagi* 'pasture' + *nes* 'headland'
St. Allen	Eglosalan	KH	'church of Saint Alan' *Eglosellan* 1840
Altarnon	Alternonna	KH	'altar of Saint Nonna'
St. Anthony in Meneage	Lannentenin	KH	'holy-site of Saint Entenin' *Lanyntenyn* 1344
St. Anthony in Roseland	Sen Anta	NH	'Saint Anta' *St. Anthony in Roseland* 1578
Anthony	Anta	P	'personal name Anta'
St. Austell	Sen Ostell	NH	'Saint Ostell'
Baldhu 1847 formerly in Kea	Baldu	KK	'black mine-work'
St. Blazey	Lanndreth	KK	'holy-site on the beach' *Landrayth* 1284
Blisland	Blyslann	S	'a completely obscure name'
Boconnoc	Boskennek	KH	'dwelling of Kennek'
Bodmin	Bosvenegh	KK	'dwelling of monks' *Bosvenna* 1602 (Richard Carew)
Bolventor 1849 formerly in Altarnon	Bedhasbold	NN	'brave farming venture'
Botus Fleming	Bosflumyes	KM	'dwelling of Flumes'
Boyton	Trevoya	NP	'farm, settlement of Boya'

Breage	**Eglospennbro**	KKK	'church at the end of a district' *Eglospenbro* c. 1207
St. Breock	**Nanssans**	KK	'valley of a saint' *Nanssent* 1335
St. Breward	**Havosti**	NH	'summer dwelling house' *Ecclesia Sancti Brueredi de Hamathethi* c. 1180 (*Hamotedi* 1086)
Bude Haven 1836 formerly in Stratton	**Porthbud**	NM	'haven of Bud stream'
Budock	**Plywvudhek**	KH	'parish of Saint Budhek' *Plu vuthek* c.1400
St. Buryan	**Eglosveryan**	KH	'church of Saint Beryan' *Eglosberrie* 1086
Callington	**Kelliwik**	KK	'village by a grove' *Cællwic* unidentified manor
Calstock	**Kalstok**	SS	'outlying farm of Callington'
Camborne	**Kammbronn**	KK	'crooked hill' *Kameron* 1252, *Cambron* 1558
Carbis Bay 1934 formerly in Lelant	**Karrbons**	KK	'cart-bridge' the village is **Porthrepter** *Carbons* 1391
Cardinham	**Kardhinan**	KK	'camp at a hill-fort'
Carmenellis 1846 formerly in Wendron	**Karnmanalys**	KK	'rock-pile in a sheaf shape'
Chasewater 1828 formerly in Kenwyn/Kea	**Penn an Chas**	KKK	'stream of a hunt' *Penanchase* 1447
Charlestown 1847 formerly in St.Austell	**Porthmeur**	KK	'great harbour, cove' *Portmoer* 1354
St. Cleer	**Ryskaradek**	KP	'ford of Karadek' *Ecclesia Sancti Clari de Recradok* 1239
St. Clement	**Morhesk**	K	'marram grass' *Ecclesia de Moresc* 1261

St. Clether	**Sen Kleder**	NH	'Saint Kleder'
Colan	**Lannwydhek**	NK	'wooded enclosure' *Lanwithick* - Henderson
St. Columb Major	**Sen Kolomm Veur**	NPN	'great Saint Kolomm'
St. Columb Minor	**Sen Kolomm Vyghan**	NPN	'little Saint Kolomm'
Cornelly	**Gorgoes**	KK	'super wood' *Gorgoyth* c.1200, *Grugoed* 1274
Constantine	**Lanngostentin**	KH	'holy-site of Saint Kostentin' *Langustentyn* 1367
Crantock	**Lanngorrek**	KH	'holy-site of Korrek' *Lancorru* 1302
Creed	**Sen Krida**	NH	'Saint Krida' *Sancte Crida* c.1250
Crowan	**Egloskrowenn**	KH	'church of Saint Krewenn' *Eggloscrauuen* c.1170
Cubert	**Lannowynn**	KM	'holy-site of Owynn' *Lanowyn* 1622
Cuby	**Sen Kubi**	NH	'Saint Kubi' *Seint Kyby* 1555
Cury	**Egloskuri**	KH	'church of Saint Kuri' *Egloscury* 1925
Davidstow	**Lanndhewi**	NH	'holy-site of Saint Dewi'
St. Day 1833 formerly in Gwennap	**Sen Day**	NH	'Saint Day'
St. Dennis	**Dinas**	K	'hill-fort'
Devoran 1873 formerly in Feock	**Devryon**	K	'waters'
St. Dominic	**Sen Domynek**	NH	'Saint Domynek'
Duloe	**Dewlogh**	KK	'two lakes, sea-inlets'
Egloshayle	**Eglosheyl**	KK	'church estuary'
Egloskerry	**Egloskerri**	KH	'church of Saint Kerri'
Endellion	**Sen Endelyn**	NH	'Saint Endelyn' *Sancta Endelienta* 1260

St. Enoder	Eglosenoder	KH	'church of Saint Enoder' *Heglosenuder* 1086
St. Erme	Egloserm	KH	'church of Saint Erm' *Egloserm* 1345
St. Erney	Sen Erni	NH	'Saint Erni' *St. Erny* 1656
St. Erth	Lannudhno	KM	'holy-site + obscure element' *Lanuthno* 1269
St. Ervan	Sen Erven	NH	'Saint Ervan' *Seint Erven* 1397
St. Eval	Sen Uval	NK	'Saint Uval' *Sancti Uveli* 1424
St. Ewe	Lannewa	KH	'holy-site of Saint Ewa' *Lanewa* 1302
Falmouth King Charles	Aberfal Myghtern Charles	NMNN	'mouth of the River Fal'
Falmouth All Saints 1889 formerly in Budock	Oll Sens Aberfal	NNNM	'mouth of the River Fal'
Feock	Lannfiek	KH	'holy-site of Saint Fiek' *Lanfioc* c.1165
Flushing 1844 formerly in Mylor	Flushyn	S	'Vlissingen (port in Holland)
Forrabury	Krugmeur	NN	'great barrow' *Forbury* 1308
Fowey	Fowydh	KK	'beech trees' *Foath* 1602. The churchtown is **Lanngordhow** and the river **Fowi**
St. Gennys	Sen Gwynnys	NH	'Saint Gwynnys'
St. Germans	Lannaled	KM	'holy-site + obscure' *Lannaledensis* c.950 See note below.
Germoe	Sen Germow	NH	'Saint Germow' *Sent Germowe* 1549
Gerrans	Gerrens	NH	'Saint Gerrens' *St. Gerance* 1578

St. Gluvias	**Bosheydhlann**	KK	'barley field dwelling' *Behellan* c. 1500
Godolphin 1846 formerly in Breage	**Godolghan**	M	'small + obscure element'
Gorran	**Lannworon**	KH	'holy-site of Saint Goron' *Langoron* 1374
Grade	**Sen Grad**	NH	'Saint Grad' *Sancte Grade* 1347
Gulval	**Lannystli**	KM	'holy-site of Ystli' *Lanestli* 1261
Gunwalloe	**Sen Gwynnwalo**	NH	'Saint Gwynnwalo' *Sancti Winwolay* 1291
Gwennap	**Lannwenep**	KH	'holy-site of saint Gwenep' *Lamwenep* 1199 (m for nn)
Gwinear	**Sen Gwynnyer**	NH	'Saint Gwynnyer' *Sanctus Wynierus* 1286
Gwithian	**Sen Goedhyan**	NH	'Saint Goedhyan' *Sanctus Gozianus* 1327 (z for th)
Halsetown 1848 formerly in St. Ives	**Trehals**	NP	'settlement of Hals' family name
Hayle St. Elwyn 1888 formerly in Phillack	**Heyl Sen Elwyn**	KNH	'estuary + Saint Elwyn'
Helland	**Hellann**	K	'ancient enclosure'
Helston	**Hellys**	K	'ancient court'
Herrodsfoot 1851 formerly in Duloe	**Nanshiryarth**	NKK	'valley of a long ridge'
Hessenford 1834 formerly in St. Germans	**Rys an Gwraghes**	NNN	'ford of the hags'
St. Hilary	**Gorlynn**	K	'super lake' *de Gurlen* 1302
Illogan	**Egloshal**	KK	'moor land church' *Egloshal* 1302
St. Issey	**Egloskrug**	KK	'barrow church' *Eglescruke* 1382

St. Ive	Sen Iv	NP	'Saint Iv'
St. Ives	Porthia	KH	'cove, harbour of Saint Ia' *Porthia* 1291
Jacobstow	Pennalyn	KH	'end, head of Alyn' *Ecclesia Sancti Jacobi de Penalym* 1270
St. John	Sen Jowann	NP	'Saint John'
St. Juliot	Sen Julet	NH	'Saint Julet' *Seynt Julett* 1567
St. Just in Penwith	Lannyust	KH	'holy-site of Saint Yust' *Lanuste* 1396
St. Just in Roseland	Lannsiek	KH	'holy-site of Siek' *Lansioch* 1204
Kea	Lanndyge	KKH	'holy-site of thy Saint Ke' *Landege* 1311
Kenwyn	Keynwynn	KK	'white ridge'
St. Keverne	Lannaghevran	KH	'holy-site of Saint Aghevran' *Lannachebran* 1086
St. Kew	Lanndogho	KH	'holy-site of Saint Dogho' *Lannohoo* 1086
St. Keyne	Sen Keyna	NH	'Saint Keyna'
Kilkhampton	Tregylgh	nK	'farm, settlement of a round'
Ladock	Egloslask	KH	'church of Saint Lasek' *Egloslagek* 1354
Lamorran	Lannvorenn	KH	'holy-site of Saint Morenn'
Landewednack	Lanndewynnek	KKK	'holy-site of thy Saint Gwynnek'
Landrake	Lannergh	K	'clearing'
Landulph	Lanndhelek	KH	'holy-site of Saint Delek'
Laneast	Lannast	KM	'holy-site of Ast'
Lanhydrock	Lannhydrek	KH	'holy-site of Saint Hydrek'
Lanivet	Lanneves	KK	'holy-site of a sacred grove' *Lanneves* 1302
Lanlivery	Lannlivri	KH	'holy-site of Saint Livri'
Lannarth 1845 formerly in Gwennap	Lannergh	K	'clearing'

Lanreath	**Lannreydhow**	KH	'holy-site of Saint Reydhow'
Lansallos	**Lannsalwys**	KM	'holy-site of Saint Salwys'
Lanteglos by Camelford	**Nanseglos**	KK	'valley church' *Nanteglos* 1407
Lanteglos by Fowey	**Sen Wyllow**	NH	'saint Wyllow' *Ecclesia Sancti Wyllei de Lanteglos* 1284
Launcells	**Lannseles**	KM	'holy-site + obscure element'
Launceston	**Lannstefan**	KH	'holy-site of Saint Stefan'
Lawhitton	**Nansgwydhenn**	KK	'valley of a tree'
Lelant	**Lannanta**	KH	'holy-site of Saint Anta' *Lananta* c.1170
Lesnewth	**Lysnowydh**	KK	'new court'
St. Levan	**Sen Selevan**	NH	'Saint Seleven'
Lewannick	**Lannwenek**	KH	'holy-site of Saint Gwenek' *Lanwenuc* c. 1125
Lezant	**Lannsans**	KK	'holy-site of Sans' *Lansant* c. 1125
Linkinhorne	**Lanngynhorn**	KH	'holy-site of Saint Kynhorn' *Lankinhorn* c. 1175
Liskeard	**Lyskerrys**	KM	'court of Kerrys'
Looe 1709 formerly in St. Martin by Looe	**Logh**	K	'lake'
Lostwithiel	**Lostwydhyel**	KK	'tail of wooded area'
Ludgvan	**Lusowan**	K	'ashes place'
Luxulyan	**Logsulyen**	KH	'cell of Sulyen'
Mabe	**Lannvab**	KH	'holy-site of Mab' *Lavabe* 1524
St. Mabyn	**Sen Mabon**	NH	'Saint Mabon'
Madron	**Eglosvadern**	KH	'Church of Saint Madern' *Eglosmaddarn* 1370
Maker	**Magor**	K	'ruin'
Manaccan	**Managhan**	KK	'place of monks' *la Ministre* 1360

Marazion 1813 formerly in St. Hilary	**Marghasyow**	KK	'Thursday market'
Marhamchurch	**Eglosvarwenn**	NP	'church of Saint Marwenn'
St. Martin by Looe	**Penndrumm**	KK	'end of a ridge' *Sancti Martini de Pendrim* 1318
St. Martin in Meneage	**Didemin**	NH	'unknown saint's name' *Didemin* 1384
St. Martin (Scilly)	**Breghyek**	K	'place of arms' *Brethiek* 1336, *Brechiek* 1390
St. Mary (Scilly)	**An Nor**	KK	'the ground' *Ennore* 1193
Mawgan in Meneage	**Sen Mowgan**	NH	'Saint Mowgan' *Seynt Mowgan* 1470
Mawgan in Pydar	**Lannhorn**	KH	'holy-site of obscure element' *Sanctus Mauchanus of Lanherno* 1257
Mawnan	**Sen Mownan**	NH	'Saint Mownan' *Seynt Maunan* 1398 Mawnan Smith is **Mownan an Gov**
St. Mellion	**Sen Melyan**	NH	'Saint Melyan'
Menheniot	**Mahunyes**	Kh	'plain of Hunyes'
St. Merryn	**Sen Meryn**	NH	'Saint Meryn' *Seynt Meryn* 1379
Merther	**Eglosverther**	KK	'church of place of relics' *Eglosmerther* 1327
Mevagissey	**Lannvorek**	KK	'holy-site of coastal area' *Lammorech* c.1210
St. Mewan	**Sen Mewen**	NH	'Saint Mewan' *Seynt Mewen* 1397
St. Michael's Mount 1859 formerly in St. Hilary	**Karrek Loes yn Koes**	KKKK	'grey rock in the wood' *Carrack Looes en Cooes* c. 1675. See note below

St. Michael Caerhays	Lannvighal	KH	'holy-site of Saint Mighal' *Lanvyhayll* 1473
St. Michael Penkivel	Pennkevyll	KK	'end, head of a horse' *Penkevel* c.1210
Michaelstow	Lannvighal	NH	'holy-site of Saint Mighal'
Millbrook 1867 formerly in Maker	Govermelin	NN	'mill stream'
Minster	Talkarn	KK	'hill brow of a rock-pile'
St. Minver	Sen Menvra	NH	'Saint Menra'
Mithian 1848 formerly in St. Agnes	Mydhyen	M	'an obscure name'
Morvah	Morvedh	KK	'sea grave'
Morval	Morval	M	'an obscure name'
Morwenstow	Lannvorwenna	NH	'holy-site of Saint Morwenna'
Mount Hawke 1847 formerly in St. Agnes	Menydhhok	NN	'hillside of hawke' (family name)
Mullion	Eglosvelyan	KH	'church of Saint Melyan *Eglosmeylyon* 1342
Mylor	Lannwydhek	KK	'Saint Melor' *Lanwydhek* 1925 Mylor Bridge is **Ponsnowydh**
St. Neot	Lanniet	NH	'holy-site of Saint Niet' *Nietestou* 1086
Newlyn East	Eglosniwlin	KM	'church of Saint Niwlin' *Eglosnyulin* 1415
Newlyn St. Peter 1851 formerly in Paul	Lulynn Sen Peder	KKNP	'fleet pool' *Lulyn* 1290
Newquay 1882 formerly in St. Columb Minor	Tewynn Pleustri	KM	'sand dune + obscure element' *Tewen blustry* 1440
North Hill	Bre Gledh	NN	'north hill'
North Petherwin	Pederwynn Gledh	HKN	'north + blessed Saint Peder'

North Tamerton	Tre war Damer	NAK	'farm, settlement on the River Tamar'
Otterham	Sen Tenia	NH	'obscure saint's name' *St. Tenye* 1613
Padstow	Lannwedhenek	KH	'holy-site of Saint Gwedhenek' *Lanwethenek* 1350
Par 1849 formerly in St. Blazey and Tywardreath	An Porth	NK	'the cove, harbour' *Le Pare* 1573
Paul	Brewynni	KS	'hill + obscure' *Sanctus Paulus of Breweny* 1323
Pelynt	Plywnennys	KH	'parish of Saint Nennys'
Pencoys 1881 formerly in Wendron	Pennkoes	KK	'end, head of a wood'
Pendeen 1849 formerly in St. Just in Penwith	Penndin	KK	'end, head of hill-fort'
Penponds 1854 formerly in Camborne	Pennpons	KK	'end, head of bridge'
Penwerris 1848 formerly in Budock	Pennweres	KK	'end, head of soil'
Penzance St. Mary 1789 formerly in Madron	Pennsans Sen Maria	KKNH	'holy end, head + Saint Maria'
Penzance St. John 1881 formerly in Madron	Pennsans Sen Jowann	KKNH	'holy end, head + Saint Jowann'
Penzance St. Paul 1867 formerly in Madron	Pennsans Sen Pawl	KKNH	'holy end, head + Saint Pawl'
Perranarworthal	Pyran ar Woethel	HKK	'Saint Pyran next to a water course'

Perranuthnoe	**Pyranudhno**	HM	'Saint Pyran +obscure element'
Perranzabuloe	**Pyran yn Treth**	KKK	'Saint Pyran in the beach' *Pirran in Treth* 1425
Little Petherick	**Nansfenten**	KK	'valley of a spring' *Nanfonteyn* 1281
Phillack	**Sen Felek**	NH	'Saint Felek' The churchtown is Eglosheyl, *Egglosheil* c.1170
Philleigh	**Eglosros**	KK	'church of heath land' *Sanctus Filius of Eglosros* 1312
Pillaton	**Trebeulyow**	nN	'farm, settlement of posts'
St. Pinnock	**Sen Pynnek**	NH	'Saint Pynnek'
Porthleven 1846 formerly in Sithney/Breage	**Porthleven**	KK	'cove, harbour of smooth stream'
Port Isaac 1913 formerly in St. Endellion	**Porthusek**	KM	'cove, harbour + obscure element' *Portusek* 1337
Poughill	**Fentenvoekka**	NN	spring of a goblin'
Poundstock	**Tregorlann**	nNN	'farm, settlement of a cattle enclosure'
Probus	**Lannbroboes**	KH	'holy-site of Saint Proboes' *Lanbrebois* 1086
Quethiock	**Gwydhek**	S	'wooded area' See note below
Rame	**Penn an Hordh**	KKK	'end, head of the ram' *Pend en Har* c.1675 See note below
Redruth St. Uny	**Rysrudh Sen Uni**	KKNH	'red ford + Saint Uni'
Redruth St. Andrew 1884 formerly in Redruth St. Uny	**Rysrudh Sen Androw**	KKNH	'red ford + Saint Andrew'
Roche	**An Garrek**	KK	'the rock' *La Roche* 1258
Ruan Lanihorne	**Lannrihorn**	KH	'holy-site of Rihorn'

Ruan Major	Ruan Veur	HN	'great Saint Ruan'
Ruan Minor	Ruan Vyghan	HN	'little Saint Ruan'
Saltash 1697 formerly in St. Stephen by Saltash	Essa	K	'ash' *Esse* 1201 Norman French *esse* 'ash' See note below
St. Sampson	Goelnans	KK	'festival valley' *Golenance* 1454
Sancreed	Eglossankres	KH	'church of Saint Sankres' *Egglossanres* 14443
Sennen	Sen Senana	NH	'Saint Senen' *Sancta Senana* 1327
Sheviock	Seviek	K	'strawberry patch'
Sithney	Merthersydhni	KH	'place of relics of Saint Sydhni' *Merthersitheny* 1230
South Hill	Bre Dheghow	NN	'south hill'
South Petherwin	Pederwynn Dheghow	HKN	'south + blessed Saint Peder'
St. Stephen in Brannel	Eglosstefan	KH	'church Saint Stefan' *Eglostephen* 1578
St. Stephen by Launceston	Sen Stefan	KPN	'holy-site of Saint Stefan'
St. Stephen by Saltash	Treveu	KS	'farm, settlement + ?' *Ecclesia Sancti Stephani de Tremeton* 1284
Stoke Climesland	Eglosstok	KK	'church of outlying farm' *Church of Stoke* 1266
Stratton	Strasnedh	KK	'wide valley of River Nedh' *Strætneat* c. 880
Stithians	Sen Stedhyans	NH	'Saint Stedhyans' *Seynt Stedyan* 1478
Talland	Tallann	KK	'hill-brow enclosure'
St. Teath	Eglostedha	KH	'church of Saint Tedha' *Egglostetha* c.1190
Temple	Tempel	K	'temple'
St. Thomas by Launceston	Sen Tommas	NH	'Saint Tommas' *St. Thomas by Launceston* 1595

Tideford 1845 formerly in St. Germans	**Rystydi**	NS	'ford of the River Tydi (Tiddy)'
Tintagel	**Tre war Venydh**	KKK	'farm, settlement on a hillside' *Trewarvene* 1259 Tintagel itself is **Dintagell**
Torpoint 1819 formerly in Anthony	**Penntorr**	KK	'end, head of a crag'
Towednack	**Tewynnek**	KH	'thy Saint Gwynnek'
Tregony	**Trerigni**	KH	'farm, settlement of Rigni'
Treleigh 1871 formerly in Redruth St. Uny	**Trelegh**	KK	'farm, settlement of a slab'
Tremaine	**Treven**	KK	'farm, settlement of stone'
Treneglos	**Treneglos**	KKK	'farm, settlement of the church'
Tresco (Scilly)	**Treskaw**	KK	'farm, settlement of elder trees'
Treslothan 1845 formerly in Camborne	**Tresulwedhen**	KH	'farm, settlement of Sulwedhen' *Tresulwethen* 1356
Tresmere	**Trewasmeur**	KH	'farm, settlement of Gwasmeur'
Trevalga	**Trevelgi**	KH	'farm, settlement of Melgi'
Treverbyn 1850 formerly in St. Austell	**Treverbin**	KH	'farm, settlement of Erbin'
Trewen	**Trewynn**	KK	'white farm, settlement'
Truro St. Mary	**Truru Sen Maria**	MNH	'obscure name + Saint Maria'
Truro St. George 1847 formerly in Truro St. Mary	**Truru Sen Jori**	MNH	'obscure name + Saint Jori'
Truro St. John 1852 formerly in Truro St. Mary	**Truru Sen Jowann**	MNH	'obscure name + Saint Jowann'
Truro St. Paul 1865 formerly in Truro St. Mary	**Truru Sen Pawl**	MNH	'obscure name + Saint Pawl'

Tuckingmill 1845 formerly Camborne	**Melindrukkya**	KK	'tucking mill'
St. Tudy	**Eglostudi**	KH	'church of Saint Tudi' *Hecglostudic* 1086
Tywardreath	**Chi war Dreth**	KKK	'house on a beach'
St. Veep	**Sen Vep**	NH	'Saint Vep' *Seynt Vep* 1407
Veryan	**Elerghi**	KK	'swans river' *Elerchi* 1086
Warbstow	**Lannwarburgh**	NP	'holy-site of Saint Warburgh'
Warleggan	**Gorlegan**	MM	'super + obscure element'
Week St. Mary	**Gwig Sen Maria**	KNN	'village of Saint Maria'
Wendron	**Egloswendron**	KH	'church of Saint Gwendron' *Eglosiga* 1208
St. Wenn	**Sen Gwenna**	NH	'Saint Gwenna'
Werrington	**Trewolvrin**	Np	'farm, settlement of Wolvrin'
Whitstone	**Mengwynn**	NN	'white stone'
St. Winnow	**Sen Gwynnow**	NH	'Saint Gwynnow'
Withiel	**Gwydhyel**	K	'wooded area'
Zennor	**Eglossenara**	KH	'Saint Senara' *Zennor Churchtown* otherwise *Eglos Senor* 1781, *Sancta Senara* 1270

The Cornish word Sen

The most common new translation, code N, is Cornish **Sen** for English 'Saint.' Thus Mylor is given the Cornish form **Sen Melor**, the **Sen** being justified by the historic form *Seint Melor* 1270. So Colan, Gwinear and Kea become **Sen Kolan, Sen Gwynnyer** and **Sen Ke**. As well as being historically more accurate this helps prevent false interpretation of personal names such as Colan being derived from **kollenn** 'hazel tree', Gwinear from **gwynn yer** 'white hens' or Kea as **ke** 'hedge.'

Assibilance

This is the change of the sound /d/, written <d> or <t>, to /z/, written <s>. This change occurred in the twelfth century and can be seen in many place-names in Mid and West Cornwall e.g. Bissoe (Kea) was *Bedow* c.1250 and *Besow* 1480. The medial <d> has become <s>. Forms on today's map that show a final <t> or <d> were thought to indicate that the language had died out in that region i.e. east of Bodmin.

However research by Julyan Holmes of **Kesva an Taves Kernewek** has clearly shown that the language had not died out in East Cornwall but assibilance had occurred however the place-name had reverted to an older form. Liskeard was *Liscarret* 1086 (final <t>) then *Liskyrres* 1298 (final <s>) before reverting to an older form that gives us the modern map form with of Liskeard with its final <d>. Thus forms such as **Bosflumes** are given for Botusfleming which derives from **bos** 'dwelling' and the personal name *Flemet* are given. Menheniot is derived from **ma** 'plain' + **Hunyet** 'a personal name' but the Cornish is **Mahunyes**. The exception to this is St. Germans, **Lannaled** in Cornish, as the same element appears in unassibilated form as Allet near Truro.

Compounds

The Cornish **hellann** is derived from **hen** 'ancient' + **lann** 'enclosure' and **hellys** derived from **hen** + **lys** 'court' are considered here as being a single word. Thus Helland **Hellann** is given the code K instead of KK as elsewhere.

English double names

One advantage that the Cornish forms have is that parishes with the same English name are easily differentiated. Thus St. Just in Penwith and St. Just in Roseland in their Cornish forms become **Lannyust** and **Lannsiek** respectively. Similarly Lanteglos by Camelford and Lanteglos by Fowey become **Nanseglos** and **Sen Wyllow**, St. Martin by Looe and St. Martin in Meneage become **Sen Martin** and **Didemin** and also the parishes of St. Mawgan in Meneage and St. Mawgan in Pydar are **Sen Mowgan** and **Lannhorn**. A triple name exists in St. Stephen; St. Stephen in Brannel, St. Stephen by Launceston and St. Stephen by Saltash but using the historic forms the names of these parishes in Cornish are; **Eglosstefan, Sen Stefan** and **Treveu**.

Anomalies

Callington/**Kelliwik** - the Cornish form takes its form from an unidentified manor formerly *Cællwic* and *Cællincg* but the form **Kelliwik** has gained currency of usage by Cornish speakers over the last fifty years or so.

Quethiock/**Gwydhek** - although derived from Cornish **koesek** 'wooded' is known as **Gwydhek** because this better fits the distortion of the name found on today's map.

Rame/**Penn an Hordh** - again this is a modern spelling of an old translation, namely William Scawen's *Pend en Har* 'end, head of a ram.' This meaning is not secure but Scawen's interpretation is taken at face value here.

Saltash/**Essa** - this is known widely and for some time in Cornish as **Essa**. This is an alternative form derived from Norman French but a truer translation of the meaning, say **Trevonnenn**, would be hard pressed to replace the established form, **Essa**. Henderson has the Cornish form for Saltash as **Essa** in *The Cornish Church Guide*, published in 1925.

St. Michael's Mount/**Karrek Loes yn Koes** - this is given the name **Karrek Loes in Koes** in Cornish and it is itself derived from a fanciful name give to the mount by gentlemen antiquarians in the seventeenth century.

Torpoint/**Penntorr** – this has the Cornish form **Penntorr** which comprises of two elements **penn** 'head, end' and **torr** meaning 'belly' and not 'crag' or such which would be better rendered as **karn**. However the Cornish **torr** is near enough to be regarded as a valid translation.

Today the place-names of Cornish parishes provide a whole mythology of fantastic miracles and martyrdom of Celtic saints. They remind us of our links with Wales, Brittany and Ireland and provide the basis for renewed interest in Cornish heritage, language and culture.

Thanks

Meur ras to the many members **Kesva an Taves Kernewek**/The Cornish Language Board whose collective knowledge of, and about, the Cornish Language is unsurpassed. **Meur ras** also to my wife, Jane, who checks my English.

PH

Select Bibliography

Henwyn Tyller Yn Kernow – Place Names In Cornwall, George, Hodge, Holmes & Sandercock, Kowethas an Yeth Kernewek, 1995.

The New Standard Cornish Dictionary – An Gerlyver Kres, Dr. Ken George, Kesva an Taves Kernewek, 1998.

A Popular Dictionary of Cornish Place-Names, O.J. Padel, Alison Hodge, 1988.

The Place Names of Cornwall, J. Gover, Unpublished, 1948.

The Cornish Church Guide, C. Henderson, Oscar Blackford, 1925.

Cornish Names, P. Hodge, Kesva an Taves Kernewek, 2001.

A Book of the West, Sabine Baring Gould, Metheun & Co, 1899.

The Isles, Norman Davies, Macmillan, 1999.

Kingdoms of the Celts, John King, Blandford, 2000.

The Cornish Language and its Literature, Peter Berresford Ellis Routledge & Kegan Paul, 1974.

Language and History in Early Britain, Kenneth Jackson, Four Courts Press, 1953.

Early Monasteries in Cornwall, Lynnette Olson, Boydell, 1989

A Map of the Ecclesiastical Parishes in Cornwall, Cornwall County and Diocesan Record Office, 1990.

Rag kedhlow yn kever an taves kernewek kestav orth
For further information about Cornish contact;

Soedhek Dyllansow ~ The Board's Publications Officer:

✉ Jori Ansell
    65 Churchtown
    Gwinear
    HEYL/HAYLE
    Kernow TR27 5JL

☎   01736 850878
E   jori.ansell@virgin.net

Skrifennyades Kemmyn ~ The Board's General Secretary:

✉ Maureen Pierce
    16 Trelawny Rd
    KELLIWIK/CALLINGTON
    Kernow PL17 7EE

☎   01579 382511
E   mpiercekernow@hotmail.com

Skrifennyades Apposyansow ~ The Board's Examinations Secretary:

✉ Maureen Fuller
    11 Barton Close
    Landrake
    ESSA/SALTASH
    Cornwall PL12 5BA

☎   01752 851552
E   mfuller@brunel.cornwall.sch.uk

BEATING THE BIG END OF TOWN

How a community defeated the East-West toll road

Published in Melbourne by the Socialist Party
PO BOX 1015 Collingwood, Victoria, Australia, 3066
Email: info@socialistpartyaustralia.org
Web: www.sp.org.au
Phone: +61 3 9639 9111

Editing, typesetting and cover design by: Mel Gregson
Front cover illustration: Michelle Baginski
Back cover photo: Oliver Marras

Printed by: Lightning Source, Melbourne
First edition May 2015

Copyright 2015 (c) Socialist Party
ALL RIGHTS RESERVED

No part of this publication may be reproduced, stored in a retrieval system or transmitted, in any form or by any means, electronic, mechanical, photocopying, recording, or otherwise, without the prior permission of the publisher.

National Library of Australia Cataloguing-in-Publication entry:

Main, Anthony.
Beating the big end of town: How a community defeated the East-West toll road / By Anthony Main

ISBN: 9780646934525 (paperback)

Subjects: Highway bypasses-Victoria-Melbourne-Public opinion. Express highways-Victoria-Melbourne-Public opinion. Pressure groups-Victoria-Melbourne. Civil rights and socialism-Victoria-Melbourne. Socialism-Victoria-Melbourne. Philosophy, Marxist-Victoria-Melbourne. Marxian economics-Victoria-Melbourne. Road construction industry-Privatisation-Victoria-Melbourne. East-West Link (Melbourne, Vic.) Australia-Politics and government,-2001-.

Dewey Number: 388.122099451

CONTENTS

About the author	**4**
Acknowledgements	**5**
Introduction	**7**
1. Behind the toll road push	**11**
2. Preparing the ground for action	**21**
3. Battle begins to heat up	**35**
4. Targeting the profiteers	**49**
5. Direct action turns situation	**63**
6. Building up political pressure	**81**
7. The election and campaign victory	**93**
8. Planning for people not profits	**105**
Timeline	**113**
Song: No Tunnel No Way	**117**
About the Socialist Party	**118**

ABOUT THE AUTHOR

Anthony Main has been a National Organiser for the Socialist Party since 2005 and has lived in the inner northern suburbs of Melbourne since the late 1990s.

He has been involved in many community campaigns in the area over that time and between 2010 and 2012 he was a Socialist Party councillor at the City of Yarra.

He first became involved in the campaign against the East-West toll road in 2008 as a founding member of the group YCAT (Yarra Campaign Against the Tunnel).

In 2013 he helped organise the first community picket against the test drilling for the project and from then until the campaign was successful he became the coordinator of what became known as the Tunnel Picket group.

Throughout the course of the dispute he was one of the key organisers and spokespeople for the campaign.

ACKNOWLEDGEMENTS

While my name is on the cover this book would not have been possible without the work of Mel Gregson. Mel made many important changes to this book that vastly improved upon my initial draft. She also designed the cover artwork and did the typesetting and layout. Her contribution to both the struggle against the East-West Link, and to this publication, was indispensable.

I would also like to thank Kevin McLoughlin, Stephen Jolly and Chris Dite for reading the drafts of this book and making suggestions about the content and style. Thanks also to Simon Strong for proof reading the final draft. Any mistakes which remain I take full responsibility for.

The Socialist Party welcomes and encourages comments, feedback and discussion about the ideas outlined in this publication. We look forward to other people telling their stories about this important struggle.

Anthony Main, May 2015

INTRODUCTION

"We beat the East-West toll road!" announced the poster plastered across Melbourne's inner-north in early December 2014. It was an open invitation to a victory street party celebrating the success of one of the most important community campaigns in recent history. To achieve this incredible victory we overcame a number of major hurdles to beat the big end of town.

From the outset the East-West toll road was a project designed to serve the needs of big business, not ordinary people. The fight to stop it from being built was a dispute between the majority of Victorians and a tiny number of shareholders of the global companies set to profit off this monster road. Representing the profiteers was an arrogant state government, eventually thrown from power for backing the project right up until its final days.

The campaign to stop the East-West toll road took place against the backdrop of a deteriorating economic situation in Australia and across the world. Australia had initially been sheltered from the worst of the world economic crisis that began in 2008 by a long-running boom in the mining sector. In the years following, as it became clear that the mining boom was coming to an end, Australian big business and its political representatives began looking for new, highly-profitable outlets for their capital. This was the primary motivation behind the push for Australia's largest ever infrastructure project - the East-West toll road.

With Australia's manufacturing sector in rapid decline, many business strategists were pushing for major investment in infrastructure projects – particularly roads that benefited the big transport firms.

Toll roads are attractive to investors as they offer multiple layers of profiteering, first during the construction phase and later through the operation of the road. In the case of the East-West toll road the operation would be underwritten by taxpayers, meaning that Victorians would cover any shortfalls in profits over the life of the road. According to the government's own figures, this would amount to billions of dollars in handouts for big business for decades into the future. Those who actually used the road would also pay again through expensive tolls.

The project would swallow decades' of transport funding into one monstrous road, leaving Melbourne's underfunded and aging public transport network in dire straits. Making matters worse, dozens of homes would need to be knocked down and the historic Royal Park - Melbourne's largest inner-city park – would be carved up to make way for the new road. The project threatened to irrevocably change the face of the city and destroy heritage sites in Melbourne's inner-north.

It was primarily for these reasons that the Socialist Party dubbed the project a social, environmental and economic disaster.

With scant resistance to their pro-big business agenda on other fronts, cocky state and federal governments expected to face little serious opposition to the East-West toll road. They were wrong.

We were able to build a strong community campaign that brought to light the real motivations behind the East-West toll road and, most importantly, prepared thousands of people to actively resist its construction.

In the process of stopping the East-West toll road we helped throw an arrogant government out of office, halted the transfer of billions of dollars of public money into the coffers of big business and emphasised the need for massive investment in public transport as an alternative to privately operated toll roads.

When we started very few people believed we could win. The Socialist Party saw the potential in an angry - yet largely dormant - community and a widespread disaffection with the pro-big business policies of the major political parties. Most Victorians want better public transport yet funding has been denied for decades. Recent large infrastructure projects in the state had proven disastrous, making people suspicious of government intentions. Concern about climate change remained strong, but no serious policy was being put forward to address the problem. In these conditions we understood a successful challenge to the East-West toll road was possible.

However, the outcome of this battle was never pre-determined. Decades of economic boom had made an impact on political consciousness. When things appear to be improving for everyone, the contrary and competing interests of the wealthy elite and ordinary people are downplayed. With the tide of Australia's economic fortunes changing, people who once felt that politics had a minimal impact on their lives begin taking more of an interest. This however is never a straightforward process.

Across the world governments are proving themselves incapable of meeting the basic needs of the world's population, all the while enriching themselves and their allies through their positions of power. We have entered an era of austerity for the billions and an unimagined accumulation of wealth for the billionaires. Ordinary people everywhere are being pushed into struggles over how society's wealth is distributed, to defend themselves and their standards of living. Through this the lessons, ideas and politics of struggle are being relearned.

10   BEATING THE BIG END OF TOWN

It is in this context that socialist ideas have found renewed relevance internationally. Through the Socialist Party these ideas informed the campaign strategy that allowed us to defeat the East-West toll road. Through this struggle these ideas gave a glimpse of what can be achieved when ordinary people come together and fight for our collective interests.

This book is not an attempt at a thorough history of the dispute. Far too much occurred to fit it all here. It is instead a brief overview of some of the key aspects of the community campaign. It has been written from the political perspective of the Socialist Party – an organisation that played a leading role throughout the life of the dispute. Our hope is that others standing up to big business interests will take inspiration from this win and draw lessons from our experience that can lead to further victories.

One of the community pickets that stopped the East-West toll road in Melbourne. Image: Brune Goguillon

CHAPTER 1
BEHIND THE TOLL ROAD PUSH

The proposed East-West Link was an 18-kilometre toll road to be built across Melbourne's inner-north. The first stage was to be a $10 billion tunnel that connected the Eastern Freeway to CityLink. Stage two was an above ground road that continued to the Western Ring Road.

The combined cost of both stages of the project was estimated to be around $18 billion. This would make it one of the most expensive infrastructure projects in the world, and the largest in Australian history.

The East-West Link was planned first and foremost as a commercial freight link. The road would have provided a more direct route for trucks to the Port of Melbourne. While the public was to foot the bill for the East-West Link through taxes and tolls, it was the mega firms like Toll Holdings, Linfox and Caltex that would have been the main beneficiaries.

To build the road more than a hundred homes would have been acquired and demolished, mostly at the eastern end. Some of the residents who faced being forced out of their homes had lived in the area for decades. Siblings Keith Fitzgerald and Faye Ryrie, both retired, were set to lose the home that their family had lived in for seventy years, an old Victorian cottage on Bendigo Street, Collingwood.

Huge sections of Royal Park in Parkville - home to rare native parkland and many sporting clubs - were to be destroyed to make way for a Los Angeles style "spaghetti junction": a tangled, concrete mess of on and off ramps.

These controversies led to immediate opposition to the project. When the East-West toll road was touted by the Labor Government in 2008, community groups were formed to oppose it. One of those was the Yarra Campaign Against the Tunnel (YCAT). YCAT grew out of a public meeting initiated by the Socialist Party and our local councillor Stephen Jolly. In 2008 the group organised several public meetings and protests including a rally at Smith Reserve in Fitzroy, near the mouth of the proposed tunnel.

In the aftermath of the 2008 global financial crisis, the then Labor government had trouble getting private investors interested in the tunnel section of the project. With this uncertainty, as well as the certainty of public opposition, the project was put on the backburner.

It wasn't until years later, in May 2013, that the new Liberal Premier Denis Napthine announced a revival of the project. His government planned to proceed with the tunnel at the eastern end. Without consulting the community, Premier Napthine announced that construction would start before the next Victorian state election scheduled for November 2014. The East-West toll road would become Napthine's defining policy; the project he believed could win him re-election.

In September 2013 the Liberal Party also came to power at a federal level. Prime Minister Tony Abbott gloated that he wanted to be known as the "infrastructure Prime Minister". At a federal and state level Abbott and Napthine promoted the East-West Link in tandem, claiming that it would create jobs and be a boon for commuters. Abbott pledged $3 billion of federal money towards the project with the state government committing a further $2 billion. The rest of the initial construction costs would come from

BEHIND THE TOLL ROAD PUSH   13

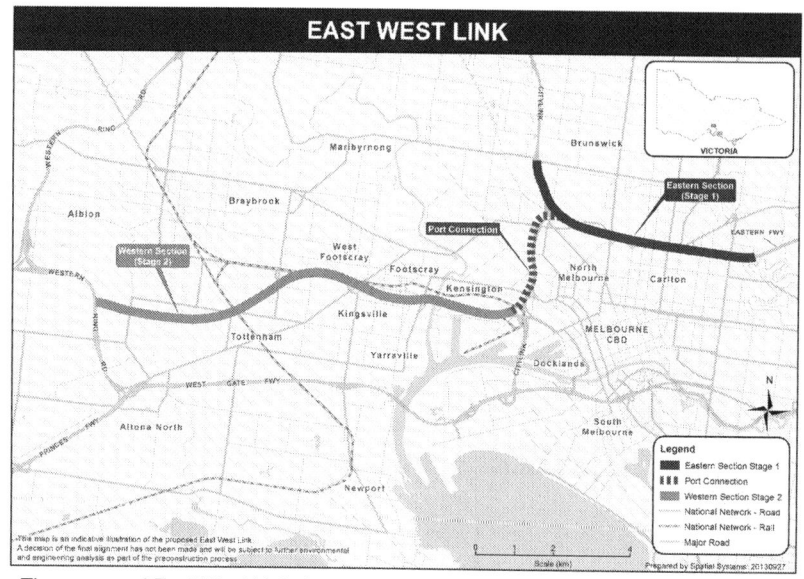

The proposed East-West Link. Image: Australian government budget papers

a private consortium that would bid for the contract to build and operate the toll road.

However, the costs to taxpayers would not end there. The government proposed a specific type of public-private partnership arrangement that guaranteed fixed quarterly payments to the toll road operator no matter how many vehicles used the road. This totally minimised the risk for private investors, ensuring massive profits regardless of the road's performance. This arrangement resulted from the fact that the numbers needed to justify the project – the projections regarding how many cars would actually use a road primarily designed as a commercial freight route – simply did not add up.

It has been an ongoing trend in recent years for toll road projections to be grossly inflated. This initially helps projects to get the go ahead, but causes problems for investors when toll revenues do not materialise. With the East-West Link profits would be guaranteed at a massive expense to taxpayers. In an attempt to hide this rort the government planned to keep the business case – the supposed rationale for the project - secret.

The Liberals were keen to hide the fact that this arrangement amounted to an enormous government handout to some of the world's largest corporations. While these firms cashed in their billions, Victorian taxpayers and commuters would be left with an enormous white elephant. The Liberals had overcome the roadblock the previous Labor government had faced in terms of attracting investment.

ENTIRE ESTABLISHMENT BEHIND THE LINK

The entire political and business establishment supported the East-West toll road, on these outrageous terms. Both the major political parties wanted the toll road built. This bipartisan support was echoed in the pages of the mainstream press. Even the majority of the trade unions were in favour of it, due to their close ties to the Labor Party and their reluctance to push for alternative infrastructure projects that would benefit Victorian workers and create sustainable, skilled jobs.

Despite the many strong arguments against the East-West toll road, the initial political consensus meant the fight to stop it was going to be an uphill battle.

The Socialist Party knew that successfully rallying a large number of people against the project would require a multitude of approaches, including challenging key aspects of the government's economic agenda, outlining a pro-worker alternative to Melbourne's transport problems, directing people's concern over climate change into opposition to the East-West toll road, and reintroducing the notion of direct community action.

One thing in our favour was the growing instability in the Australian political system. Federally, the Abbott Liberal government had come to power not out of popularity, but in a wave of backlash against previous Labor governments. Before its election the Abbott government had stated few concrete policies, and denied an agenda of anti-worker cuts and privatisations. The deteriorating economic situation made sure that the new government's first budget would prove this a shameless lie. Frustration with the two major political parties had also handed Abbott an unpredictable minority senate.

In Victoria, the first term Napthine Liberal government was struggling in the polls, having already changed leaders mid-term. Napthine had a mere one seat majority in the parliament and faced an election in a little over a year.

The Victorian Liberal government had already shown its weakness in March 2013, when the Socialist Party ran a successful community campaign to stop the state sell-off of public housing land in the inner Melbourne suburbs of Fitzroy and Richmond. The plans would have meant public housing tenants would lose their precious open space to private development. Under pressure from the community campaign the government was forced into an embarrassing retreat, scrapping plans to build private apartments on public parkland worth an estimated $1 billion.

In this less-than-favourable political situation Napthine's Liberals rallied behind the East-West Link as their signature project. In what can only be understood as a combination of arrogance and a disconnect with public sentiment, the Liberal government believed it could easily win support for the East-West toll road despite initially coming to power saying it would not be built. As the Napthine government pretended to champion outer-suburban commuters and unemployed workers - all the while scheming to hand over billions in public money to corporations - an exposure of the real motivations behind the project would prove disastrous to the government's image, and re-election hopes.

16 BEATING THE BIG END OF TOWN

The potential to build a strong, tangible opposition to the East-West toll road existed; it was simply a question of how it could be done.

An important factor in the success of building the community campaign against the East-West toll road was the many years of work the Socialist Party has done in and around the area where the road would be built. Socialist Party City of Yarra councillor Stephen Jolly had a well-earned reputation as a fighter for the community after leading dozens of campaigns to save schools, parks, kindergartens and other community assets from the jaws of greedy developers.

Also in our favour was the relatively recent experience of bringing people together against the East-West Link in 2008. There was also a rich history of struggle against pro-big business road projects in the area. In the 1970s residents campaigned against the Eastern Freeway, then known as the F-19, while in the 1990s there were further struggles over the widening of Alexandra Parade. A handful of people involved in these struggles returned to the fight against the East-West toll road.

The 200 stong July 20, 2013 community meeting in Collingwood.
Image: Brune Goguillon

TESTING THE MOOD

With Premier Napthine's announcement to push ahead with the East West Link in his first term, we needed to test the mood for a renewed community campaign to stop the road. In July 2013, shortly after Napthine's announcement, the Socialist Party called a public meeting in Collingwood, near the proposed mouth of the tunnel.

Around 200 people packed into the room at the North Yarra Community Health Centre. The only planned speaker for the meeting was Socialist Party councillor Stephen Jolly. Such was the level of community frustration and anger at Premier Napthine's announcement to go ahead with the project before the next election that every local politician felt compelled to turn up.

In this historically working class but increasingly gentrified, socially diverse, politically left-leaning area of the city, all of the elected politicians claimed to be opposed to the East-West Link. Here, it would be political suicide to publicly hold any other position. It was clear to all that the East-West toll road was a major issue facing Melbourne's inner-north and nobody wanted to be left out of the discussion.

Mayor of Yarra Jackie Fristacky intervened in the meeting to try to assure residents that Yarra Council would lobby the Napthine government to change its mind. She attempted to give the impression that by participating in a sham consultation process the Council bureaucracy could resolve the matter. This position was extremely naïve at best and dishonest at worst. Her goal was to send people home believing Yarra Council, under her lead, could solve the problem on its own. She did not support the Socialist Party proposal for an active community campaign.

Greens Federal MP Adam Bandt came with one clear message: Vote Green. He claimed that the only way to stop the East-West toll

18   BEATING THE BIG END OF TOWN

road was to help the Greens win more seats at the next Victorian election, which was fourteen months away! He neglected to mention that, according to the Napthine government's schedule, the project would already be underway by then. Bandt ignored the Socialist Party proposal to build an active community campaign, instead attempting to rally people behind the Greens' electoral campaigns.

For Labor state MP Richard Wynne the meeting was tough. Labor supported the project, though Wynne attempted to position himself as an opponent. He was visibly shaking and sweating as he was booed and heckled by locals as he tried to speak – not characteristic of a man known as Labor Party "muscle" in his youth. The crux of what he said was to "stay tuned" for more information on Labor's position, indicating there may be a change in the future.

He understood more clearly than anyone that if Labor continued to support the East-West toll road, he would pay a heavy price at the next election. His seat was already a Labor/Greens marginal, with the Socialist Party steadily increasing electoral support in the area. Needless to say Wynne did not support the proposal to build an active community campaign, one that would inevitably come into conflict with himself and his party.

Subsequently we heard that Wynne was working behind the scenes to try to get Labor to modify its message. While overall Labor was keen to see the project go ahead the inner-city MPs needed to be able to go to the election pretending they opposed it.

In the following weeks Labor did modify their message somewhat. Under increasing pressure they came out saying that they were now formally opposed to the project but if the contracts were signed before the election they would honour them. This was fake opposition and it did little to console their inner-city voter base. While utterly insufficient, this attempt to trick people made Labor vulnerable. If we could build up opposition to the project it would be possible to force Labor's hand much further.

The most well-received speaker at the meeting was Socialist Party councillor Stephen Jolly. Rather than echo the narrow, self-serving electoralism of the other speakers, Jolly spoke to a larger goal. He told those at the meeting that if they wanted the project stopped, each and every one of them would have to join the campaign and fight. The Socialist Party would fight until the end, he explained, but we could not do it alone.

As a means of building active support for the campaign the Socialist Party came up with "The Pledge". The Pledge asked people to commit their support for direct action.

It read: "I pledge that I will not allow the State Government to construct the proposed East-West road tunnel. I, along with other community members, will engage in peaceful but determined direct action – including community pickets – to ensure the unpopular, costly and environmentally devastating toll road and tunnel is never built. Instead of toll roads governments should be investing in improved and expanded public transport."

After Stephen Jolly appealed to the crowd to turn their opposition into action, I presented The Pledge to the meeting. It took us by surprise how enthusiastically it was received. People understood that it was not just another petition but a strategy for collective action. They not only signed it themselves but also took hundreds of copies for friends and family to sign.

Though chaotic, the meeting marked the start of a new phase in the campaign. We followed it up with a Socialist Party organised rally at Smith Reserve in Fitzroy on August 31 and at these two events we met people who would go on to become some of the staunchest campaigners and the backbone of the struggle to stop the East-West toll road. As the government touted the project in the media, we were developing organised opposition on the ground. The foundations were being laid for the battle ahead.

Poster by Mel Gregson

SAY 'NO' TO THE EAST-WEST TUNNEL

Fight for public transport in ALL of Melbourne's suburbs!

Community action & organising is already having an effect!

Let's keep up the pressure!

RALLY: 1pm Saturday August 31 @ Smith Reserve, Fitzroy

(Corner Alexandra Pde & George St)

ORGANISED BY SOCIALIST PARTY COUNCILLOR STEPHEN JOLLY:

☎ 0437 856 713

💻 www.yarrasocialists.net

@ Stephen.Jolly@yarracity.vic.gov.au

Socialist Party australia.org

CHAPTER 2
PREPARING THE GROUND FOR ACTION

There was already significant, though latent, opposition to the tunnel amongst those who lived near the site of the project. While many people in suburban and regional areas still needed to be convinced, there was an immediate need to start to organise those who were prepared to fight. The Pledge was a tool to engage people in discussion and win them to our cause, but crucially it was also used to mobilise those people already convinced around specific goals and actions.

Through street stalls and other public activity we took the The Pledge further out into the community. It was well received and we met our initial target of 1,000 signatures within two months.

We were making modest but essential progress in cementing opposition and building support for active resistance, yet most people were speaking about the East-West toll road as a done deal. This was the message coming loud and clear from the government and through the media coverage. The approach of Labor and the Greens in directing attention solely to the next election only helped sow a feeling of helplessness amongst those opposed to the project.

Of those who were beginning to get organised there was an overwhelming focus on local issues relating to construction: the home acquisition process, questions over design details and discussions about demanding small concessions. We were continually reminding people that the project had not yet

22   BEATING THE BIG END OF TOWN

> **'NO' TO THE EAST-WEST TUNNEL**
> **'YES' TO THE DONCASTER RAIL**
>
> **I pledge** that I will not allow the state government to construct the proposed East-West road tunnel. I, along with other community members, will engage in peaceful but determined direct action - including community pickets - to ensure this unpopular, costly and environmentally devastating toll road and tunnel is never built. Instead of toll roads governments should be investing in improved and expanded public transport.
>
> | NAME | EMAIL | SIGNATURE | PHONE |
> |------|-------|-----------|-------|
> | | | | |
> | | | | |
> | | | | |
> | | | | |
> | | | | |
> | | | | |
> | | | | |
>
> For more information contact Socialist Party Councillor Stephen Jolly on 0437 856 713. Pledges can be returned to PO Box 1015 Collingwood 3066

'The Pledge' was signed by 1000 people by September 2013. Image: Mel Gregson

begun, and that direct action could stop the whole thing from going ahead. Even if we failed, we argued, the way to win the most concessions and the best deal for our community would be to mount the strongest campaign possible, giving us a better bargaining position.

Some listened to our case while others dismissed our strategy as fantastical. Despite growing support for the idea of direct action, there was still very little confidence that the project could actually be stopped.

Unfortunately there were not many recent trade union or community campaigns to point to as an example. The economic boom had successfully softened the edges of political consciousness. The unions were in decline after failing to put up any significant fight for years. The local campaigns we had initiated in recent times were far too modest compared to what would be required to stop this huge road. The examples of mass mobilisations that we based our strategy on were either foreign or distant in the past. For many, this made what we were saying somewhat abstract and hard to swallow.

THE STRATEGY

The key strategy we put forward was one of collective mass action. We argued that if we used the next year to build up an active campaign with mass support, then we could mobilise people to physically stop the construction of the East-West toll road. A daily community picket of hundreds, maybe thousands, would make the road impossible to build. Such a community stand would put us in a much stronger position to make an appeal to the unions to show solidarity and to not cross our community picket line. A stand-off of this nature would escalate quickly, with the government under pressure to either proceed with significant force and non-union labour (potentially dragging the unions and other progressive forces into the dispute), or instead to back down.

The timing of the election meant that we had real potential to win with this strategy before it even came to mass community pickets. The Liberal Party, the traditional party of big business, would likely be willing to risk an all out war with a left-leaning inner-city electorate and a weakened labour movement. The Labor Party, on the other hand, was already feeling the pressure. If we could present a credible threat of mass community action, with the potential for union support, whilst winning the public debate on the immediate need to invest in public transport, then we had a chance to make the East-West toll road a key election issue.

If we could pressure the Labor Party into vocal opposition in the lead-up to the election, it would be very difficult for a new Labor government to then turn around and build the project once elected. This is especially the case if the Labor Party believed we were capable of mobilising significant numbers of people into action if it backpedalled. After all, what's decided in parliament is merely a reflection of the balance of forces on the ground. If we could build a significant movement on the ground, then we could push the politicians into a corner and use the election to our advantage.

This strategy hinged on building the type of movement not seen in Victoria for a long time. It would not appear from nowhere, and we would have to initiate it without the unions on board. We would need to use every opportunity to demonstrate the power of collective action, to inspire people to support our fight and get involved.

Before construction could begin there was a planning process to go through, a bidding process with prospective contractors and some preliminary works to be carried out. The government had already started carrying out preliminary works, test drilling for soil samples along the proposed tunnel route.

Most of this work had been done in Royal Park and in some streets in the City of Melbourne nearer to the western end of the tunnel. There was also some important geotechnical research yet to be done in the City of Yarra, closer to the mouth of the tunnel at the eastern end.

In late September 2013, two months after the launch of The Pledge, we received information through Yarra Council about the state government's progress. The government planned to set up drill rigs in more than a dozen locations to extract soil and rock samples. These samples would be used to estimate how difficult it would be to bore the tunnel across the five-kilometre distance. This was crucial information for the construction firms to estimate their costs. The bidding process could not proceed without these samples.

The state government agency charged with overseeing the

Test drilling for soil samples before picketing commenced. Image: Mel Gregson

East-West Link, the Linking Melbourne Authority, was seeking permission from Yarra Council to set up drill rigs on council-owned streets. The Socialist Party pushed for this information to be made public.

Once we had our hands on this information, we decided the test drilling would be the first real test for the campaign. We were building up some momentum with The Pledge, but needed to determine how willing people were to actually engage in direct action.

THE CASE FOR PICKETING

At short notice the Socialist Party called a meeting in Collingwood for Sunday September 22, 2013. We planned to use the dining room of the Leinster Arms Hotel, but too many people turned up for us all to fit. We moved the meeting to across the road to the small park on Gold Street.

A new group called Residents Against the Tunnel (RAT) had been set up in the preceding weeks and we invited them to co-host the meeting. Of the thirty or so people who attended, a majority had signed The Pledge and many had been actively collecting signatures.

Stephen Jolly spoke to the meeting and explained what we knew of the test drilling schedule. He put forward the proposal to organise a community picket to stop, or at least disrupt, drilling that was taking place in Clifton Hill. People listened intently, though there was not much immediate discussion.

Two representatives from the RAT group then proceeded to read from long, pre-prepared statements about East-West Link design intricacies, the process of home acquisitions, and other details unrelated to actually stopping the East-West toll road from being built. They were speaking primarily to property owners who were weighing up their options whether to sell their houses and move on, or to hire lawyers to negotiate a better deal. A number of these homeowners were not within the acquisition zone and were deciding whether to demand that their homes be acquired or to fight to limit the impact on their properties.

While these were all valid discussion points for a specific group of residents, it became clear that there were two meetings occurring concurrently with two very different goals. The representatives from the RAT group were solely focussed on discussing issues facing property owners, while the Socialist Party wanted the meeting to focus on whether we could get agreement to call the first community picket.

This remained a common theme throughout the campaign, whereby various groups prioritised challenging certain procedural or legal aspects of the project over the campaign of direct action to stop the East-West toll road from being built. Many of these groups were focused solely on the issues facing property owners.

It was sometimes a challenge to continually find new and original ways to express the same crucial point: If we were going to win the campaign we needed to focus on the issues that impacted the millions of people across the state. If we had focused purely on the needs of a few dozen property owners, the campaign would have remained isolated, divided and been quickly defeated.

We needed a strategy that played upon the weaknesses of the overall project, coupled with tactics that hit the government where it hurts. We needed to undermine the government's own support base in the outer suburbs, support that had been built on disingenuous claims. We needed to demonstrate to all Victorians that they had a stake in the outcome of this battle by focusing on the broader social, environmental and economic issues.

Overall, we managed to convince a substantial number of people of this approach, and in turn opened up the campaign to thousands of people who otherwise may not have felt that this issue was worth their time. However, throughout the course of the next year there would be many more meetings, forums and discussions where these issues would dominate.

A genuinely democratic forum first needs to decide what it is discussing before it can facilitate that discussion in a democratic way. This was not always easy when the small groups and individuals involved were sometimes coming from vastly different understandings of what was occurring and what needed to be done.

This particular meeting in September 2013 was not the smoothest of the campaign, but after some polite interjections, the question was posed concretely: "Are you are prepared to join a community picket to stop test drilling in the coming days?" Three-quarters of those in the park raised their hands, some noticeably side-glancing those around them before committing. This provided us with the slightly timid but necessary support to begin organising for a picket of the test drilling site.

28 BEATING THE BIG END OF TOWN

A street meeting during the first week of the community picket. Image: Brune Goguillon

FIRST WEEK OF PICKETS

On Tuesday September 24, 2013 we organised the first community picket. Around fifty people turned up first thing in the morning at the drill site on the corner of Rutland Street and Alexandra Parade East in Clifton Hill. It was a cold but bright morning, and people milled around in nervous anticipation.

The drill rig itself was a big piece of equipment mounted on the back of a truck. Parked in the middle of the street over a spray painted cross to mark the spot, it was surrounded only by a few traffic cones and some flimsy safety tape.

Despite being aware of our plans, it was clear that the Linking Melbourne Authority did not see us as a serious threat. Socialist Party organiser Mel Gregson and myself first approached the two workers who arrived to operate the drill. We had checked earlier and discovered that they worked for a tiny company that did not have a union agreement. We explained to them why we were there and appealed to them to stop work in solidarity with our campaign.

We made the case that more long-term, sustainable jobs could be created by investment in public transport, and that this was what we were fighting for. They were not particularly chatty, so we ended the discussion by suggesting that they call their employer to notify them that a protest was taking place and it would be a breach of occupational health and safety standards for them to proceed with drilling. They made a call and told us that they would in fact stop work.

It was then that we convened the first meeting of picketers, to go over our goals and to relay that the workers had stopped work because of our presence. People cheered at the news, and the apprehension at the meeting two days prior started to give way to a feeling of confidence and optimism.

Collectively we made the decision to stay for as long as the workers stayed on site. An aggressive Linking Melbourne Authority supervisor turned up angered at our presence and belligerent toward us. It was he who demanded the workers stay on site, hopeful that we would leave after a few hours and drilling could resume. We waited them out in what was the government's first taste of our commitment and determination. By early afternoon the workers had gone and a skeleton crew of picketers remained to monitor the site.

From the first day we established a mode of organising that ensured decisions were made collectively. We started and ended each picket with a democratic and open street meeting where we discussed the progress of the campaign and our next plans. All major decisions would be made on the picket line by the picketers. As socialists we believe that democracy is the lifeblood of social movements. A genuine sense of ownership and control over the decision making process is necessary if we are to expect people to devote time and energy to a cause. Democratic structures ensure an open and honest appraisal of ideas and tactics, and accountability of those carrying out tasks. These conditions are necessary to build trust when working together, especially in challenging circumstances.

All groups and individuals opposed to the East-West toll road were equally welcome to participate in the process, they need only turn up. This helped ensure that no group or individual with ulterior motives could easily derail the community picket, as participating in the decision making required active involvement in the campaign.

The meeting agreed to come back again the next day, and on the days following, to continue to stop the test drilling. In a slightly convoluted and confused cross-generational discussion about the nature and use of hashtags, we settled on the very literal #TunnelPicket to help build support for our campaign on social media. From that point on the diverse group of people involved in the direct action became informally known as the "Tunnel Picket". If we'd known at the time how successful the community picket would be, we may have put a little more thought into the name.

Occupying the drilling site during first week of the community picket. Image: Brune Goguillon

ACTION BOOSTS PEOPLE'S CONFIDENCE

On day two our presence was anticipated and the two drill operators attempted to ignore us and begin drilling. We quickly convened a meeting of those present and proposed that we collectively walk into the work site and link arms in a picket around the drill. This was more confronting than the previous day, and a number of people were clearly nervous.

Determined to continue to disrupt the drilling the vast majority agreed to form a picket. This time it was only after we linked arms around the drill that the workers again stopped work. This act of unified defiance sent a clear message to the government and offered a strong visual to the TV news crews present.

Taking this modest but important first step of defiance by linking arms around the drill gave people confidence. Though boosted by the success, a number of picketers whispered nervously about what would happen when the police arrived.

When the local police inspector Bernie Edwards turned up he presented himself as a neutral observer. He said that he knew the protesters were just "ordinary mums and dads" and that he understood our frustrations. At that stage some of the less experienced activists were unclear about the role the police play defending big business interests and were taken in by Edwards' pleasantries.

While his approach was an attempt to disarm some people in the campaign it was also an indication of our strength. The police did not yet feel confident enough with the government's position to treat us with contempt. That would change in time, as did people's understanding about which side the police were actually on.

As confidence amongst the picketers grew the Linking Melbourne Authority realised that the test drilling was perhaps

Police arrive during the first week of the community picket. Image: Oliver Marras

going to be more of a headache than they had first thought. They needed to reassess their plans. We managed to disrupt all work in the first few days. The Linking Melbourne Authority reconsidered their approach and soon a fence was erected around the drill site.

We anticipated this and had a roster of people monitoring the site around the clock. However, temporary fencing can be quickly erected, and it is difficult to convene a picket in the middle of the night. After the fence went up the workers began arriving extra early to get into the site, flanked from all sides by the police.

This cut across our ability to interfere with the worksite by sheer proximity to the drilling machinery. Instead, we needed to strengthen our picket and make it impossible for the contractors to enter the site at all. This was a new situation and a much greater challenge. Though the turnout to the picket was growing each day, we did not yet have the numbers to hold our ground in the presence of dozens of police. We would need to greatly outnumber them if we were to succeed. This situation required a more serious discussion on strategy.

As the drilling recommenced on Alexandra Parade East, we

began anticipating where the next drill would be set up.

OUTREACH MODE

The most pressing task at this time was to get everyone into outreach mode. While we had been getting between 50-80 people to the pickets during the first week, we knew that opposition to the project was much deeper. More people were finding out about the pickets from coverage in the mainstream press, and we produced leaflets and posters calling on people to join our actions. However, the crucial task was to interact with people one-on-one to convince them to get involved.

We drew up a map of the proposed drill sites and doorknocked and letterboxed the surrounding areas. We called on local residents to leave their cars parked in the spots where drilling was planned and to contact us if they saw any suspicious behaviour like machinery moving in, roads being blocked off, markings on the ground or an unexpected police presence. We set up regular patrols and what we called a "rapid response team" of those who lived close by and could come to a picket at very short notice.

After tasting the success of our first week of direct action, people in the campaign had become much more committed and determined to continue. They had experienced for themselves what we had been trying to convince them of; collective community action is a powerful tool than can challenge even the most arrogant of governments. It was because of this that there was a real enthusiasm to go out and build our numbers.

34   BEATING THE BIG END OF TOWN

Poster by Mel Gregson

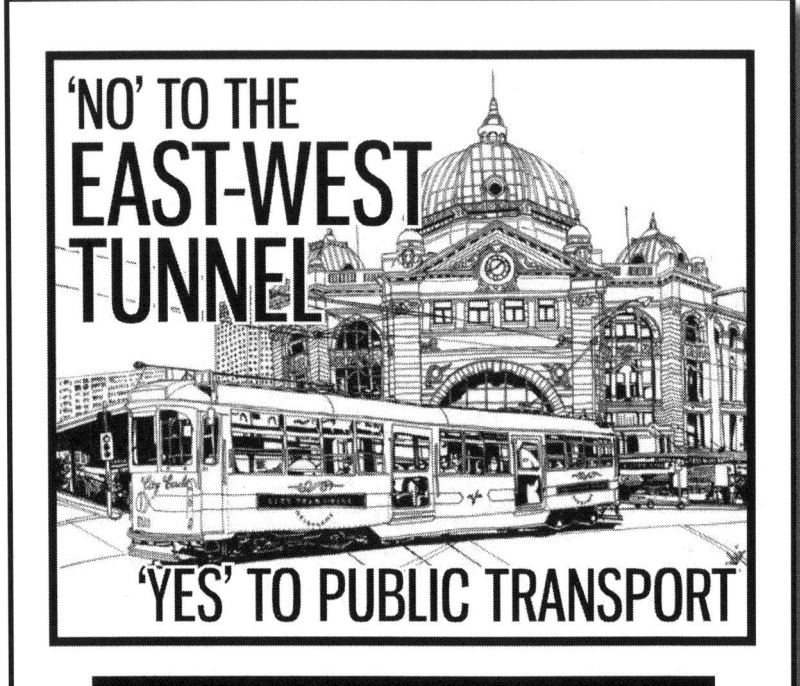

'NO' TO THE EAST-WEST TUNNEL

'YES' TO PUBLIC TRANSPORT

JOIN THE PEACEFUL COMMUNITY PICKETS TO STOP THE EAST-WEST TOLL ROAD TUNNEL

Txt 'tunnel' to 0432 447 036 to receive picket locations via txt message

CHAPTER 3
BATTLE BEGINS TO HEAT UP

By October 2013 we were engaged in a giant game of cat and mouse on the streets of Melbourne's inner-north. If residents could not leave their cars parked over the drill sites they gave us their parking permits so that we could arrange for other cars to occupy the spots. At this time nobody could walk around the area wearing as much as a fluoro vest without someone contacting us warning that works might be about to take place. Such was our reach that we got calls in the middle of the night about roadwork in areas kilometres away from the proposed site of the tunnel, just in case it was somehow related.

Unsure how to deal with our growing campaign, the Linking Melbourne Authority continued to attempt to set up drilling sites but were hindered every step of the way. On a few occasions drilling sites were set up and work progressed painfully slowly under police watch. On other days we outmanoeuvred both the Linking Melbourne Authority and the police and completely stopped all works. Every small victory was a boost to our campaign and a new headache for the government. As our numbers and successes grew, so did the police presence. By the second week of October it had become normal for a hundred police to be deployed on a given day.

With the government unwilling to deal with the political consequences resulting from a wholesale smashing of our community picket, the Linking Melbourne Authority (who by this stage had largely abandoned consultation with local residents) and police devised complicated strategies to move in equipment and contractors. On one occasion they organised a meeting place for the police escort for the drilling contractors in a suburb north of the area where test drilling was taking place. Immediately residents in that suburb notified us, and we sent people to spy on the operation. When our picketers turned up at the new drilling site moments after the police and contractors arrived, the look of exasperation on the face of the Linking Melbourne Authority executive coordinating the "secret operation" was priceless.

At every attempt to set up a new drilling site, come rain, hail or shine we would have people there forming a blockade within about fifteen minutes. Even where they managed to fence off areas of the street, we would stand in front of the entrance linking arms, sometimes three or four rows deep, to stop each piece of machinery and equipment entering the site. The only way they could get into the sites was with large numbers of police physically removing us, often one by one. Sometimes this took hours and it made every element of their work complicated and time consuming.

The slowness of the progress led the Linking Melbourne Authority to contract a second drill. This simply gave us more options for disruption, as it took the police a few attempts to figure out that we could move our picket line faster than they could move their police line. It also meant that they generally needed twice as many officers to guard the sites.

We bought an old caravan and used it to occupy one of the proposed drilling sites on the corner of Brunswick and Westgarth Streets in Fitzroy. Not only did the caravan act as a blockade, it became our campaign headquarters. We used it as a meeting place and a place to hold events and street stalls on the busy Brunswick

EAST-WEST TUNNEL DRILLING LOCATIONS

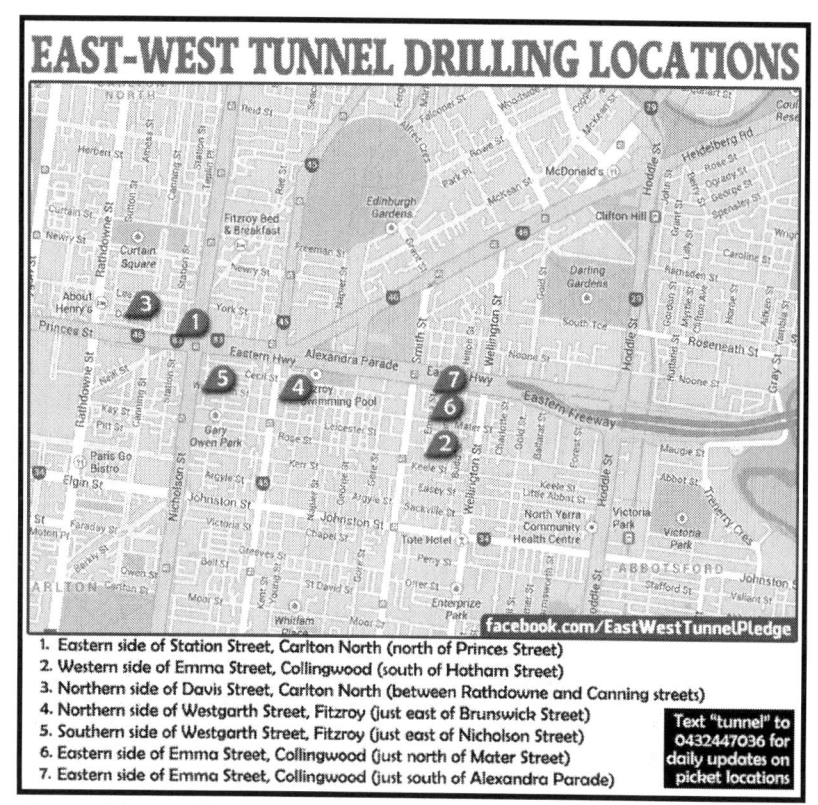

1. Eastern side of Station Street, Carlton North (north of Princes Street)
2. Western side of Emma Street, Collingwood (south of Hotham Street)
3. Northern side of Davis Street, Carlton North (between Rathdowne and Canning streets)
4. Northern side of Westgarth Street, Fitzroy (just east of Brunswick Street)
5. Southern side of Westgarth Street, Fitzroy (just east of Nicholson Street)
6. Eastern side of Emma Street, Collingwood (just north of Mater Street)
7. Eastern side of Emma Street, Collingwood (just south of Alexandra Parade)

facebook.com/EastWestTunnelPledge

Text "tunnel" to 0432447036 for daily updates on picket locations

A map of the test drilling sites we letterboxed to residents. Image: Ash Hall

Street strip.

There was huge pressure on the Linking Melbourne Authority to resolve this deadlock in order to get the project back on its tight schedule. Our pickets forced a confrontation, creating a situation whereby the government had to respond. Either they could cede to a united community and walk away, or use force to break us apart. Any illusions some picketers and supporters may have held up until this point about the police remaining neutral or secretly being on our side were smashed by the brutal reality of physical force.

Adding to the government's dilemma was the fact that every time the police used aggressive and heavy-handed tactics to drag us from drilling sites, it attracted media attention. This simply gave us further opportunity to explain to the rest of Victoria what we were doing and why, usually attracting new picketers the following day.

MAINSTREAM PRESS COVERAGE

During these first three weeks our picketing campaign began to be featured heavily in the mainstream press. Images of pensioners, students and ordinary working class people standing up to the government and defying the police became associated with the project. This represented the beginning of an important narrative shift: the idea that there was serious opposition to and a struggle against the East-West toll road.

While the mainstream media often tried to portray us as violent, this didn't wash with most people. Our picket was actually very organised and disciplined. This was reflected in hours upon hours of footage showing us standing our ground defiantly yet peacefully while the police attacked - often using underhanded tactics like pinching, groping and twisting joints - and dragged us away.

On many occasions Socialist Party members did live television and radio crosses from the pickets. While most outlets attempted to undermine our cause, or focus on the confrontations with police, we used the opportunities to speak to millions of people about the deficiency of the project and to refute the government's claims.

Our aim was never to advise or plead with the government or the Linking Melbourne Authority, or simply recite figures and statistics for the sake of it. Our aim was always to talk past the journalists and presenters to speak to their working class audiences. We attempted to take the discussion back to the central

Murdoch's Herald Sun newspaper attempted to vilify Socialist Party members on several occasions. Image: Kathleen Galea

issues: this was a project that benefited big business at the expense of ordinary people and the environment and we should instead be demanding investment in public transport.

Like the police, the mainstream media is not neutral when it comes to politics. Media corporations are themselves big businesses with their own interests and agendas. The lengths the press were prepared to go to in defence of their big business allies was shown on October 8 when the *Herald Sun* ran a front page story labelling me a "serial pest".

The *Herald Sun* story reported on the different campaigns that I had been involved with over the previous decade, presenting me as a professional protester and troublemaker. In many ways this backfired as it gave prominence to the dispute and presented me as an opponent to an unpopular government. In response I pointed out that what linked the different campaigns I had been involved with was opposition to big business domination of our lives.

The strategy of targeting certain individuals is to isolate them and cause divisions in a campaign. The Murdoch press held the false view that my identity as a socialist and long-term community campaigner would alienate me from the largely unaligned, diverse group that made up the campaign against the East-West toll road. What the editors underestimated was the amount of time the Socialist Party had put into community organising and the trust we had built up with those involved in the campaign. Almost immediately the picketers adopted the term "serial pest" as a badge of honour, proudly proclaiming that we were all serial pests and thorns in the side of the Napthine government!

While giving us some column space and airtime, the mainstream press continued to support the East-West toll road almost without exception. This was despite many of their own polls showing the majority of people were against it. Polls consistently showed that the majority of people wanted public transport prioritised over investment in the East-West Link. The polls that showed the biggest majorities against the project coincided with the height of our picketing and coverage in the press.

The community picket on Station Street, Carlton during a live TV cross. Image: Mel Gregson

THE CLASS DYNAMIC OF THE PUBLIC DEBATE

The proposed mouth of the East-West tunnel at the eastern end was situated on the border of Collingwood and Clifton Hill. Historically these are two of the oldest working class suburbs in Melbourne. In recent years rents and property prices have skyrocketed and these areas have become increasingly gentrified.

One argument the government tried to use in the press was that the people complaining about the East-West toll road were a bunch of well off middle-class "NIMBY's" (Not In My Back Yard) who were only concerned about themselves. It didn't help that some on the sidelines of the campaign were happy to reinforce this impression.

At one point a tiny but vocal minority in the campaign objected to me speaking to the media on the basis that my working class accent was not sophisticated enough to be taken seriously by the government. This (readily dismissed by others in the campaign) view represented a total misunderstanding of who we were speaking to and who we needed to seek allies amongst.

Meanwhile, Liberal government Planning Minister Matthew Guy went on the offensive, presenting the project as something that would be of great benefit to working class people in the outer suburbs. He claimed it would help reduce congestion for commuters and create jobs.

The false dichotomy of inner-city versus outer-suburbs, often implied as middle-class versus working-class, was echoed widely in the mainstream media. It was something we had to consciously undermine. We tried to use every opportunity to expose the real class dynamics behind the project, namely the way big business intended to exploit and take advantage of working class taxpayers. It became crucial for us to outline a job-creating, congestion-busting alternative to the East-West toll road.

Traffic congestion is a real problem in Melbourne and a genuine source for frustration for many in this geographically enormous and rapidly growing city. The government sought to play on this frustration (caused by their own policies) to win support for the project. We responded by focusing on the fact that investment in public transport does far more to reduce traffic congestion than building for-profit toll roads.

One of the first Socialist Party placards we made read "Public transport for ALL of Melbourne's suburbs". In interviews we always tried to explain that we wanted the money that would be wasted on the East-West toll road to be spent on public transport expansion in the suburbs of Melbourne and regional Victoria.

A much better alternative to the East-West toll road is the long-awaited rail line down the Eastern Freeway. The median strip in the centre of the Eastern Freeway was built specifically to accommodate a future rail line but successive governments, both Liberal and Labor, have refused to build it.

According to Yarra Council's Trains Not Toll Roads campaign, a rail line down the Eastern Freeway would remove 800 vehicles per peak-hour train from the road. It would service in excess of 80,000 people a day, people who currently have very poor public transport options. This, along with other major public transport extensions, would give hundreds of thousands of people the option to get out of their cars. This, in turn, would allow more room on existing roads for trucks, tradespeople and others who need to drive.

The argument about jobs being created by the East-West toll road was striking a chord with people, especially with unemployment rising in Victoria. Again, the actual figures were in our favour, with experts pointing out that investment in public transport projects creates around three times as many jobs. Unlike jobs associated with roads, these would be skilled, sustainable, long-term jobs. We also produced placards that read "Public transport = More jobs".

All of our banners and signs were aimed at speaking to the people that the government cynically looked to for a base of support. This is because we knew support for the project amongst working class people was based on lies and misinformation. Every time our picket was shown on the news we were chanting in support of public transport alternatives and holding signs calling for better public transport, sustainable jobs and socially useful infrastructure. We intended to waste no opportunity to influence public opinion in favour of our alternatives to the East-West toll road.

PROTEST TACTICS

During this period of the campaign a debate about protest tactics arose. While we were building public support for our community pickets, at best around a hundred or so people were turning up to the picket at any one time. The police presence had

Fencing was erected around the drilling sites to hinder our community pickets. Image: Sue Jackson

44   BEATING THE BIG END OF TOWN

Dozens of police surround a drilling site so work can commence. Image: Mel Gregson

begun to outnumber our presence, meaning our objectives became increasingly difficult to achieve.

Some people argued that rather than focus on picketing it would be more effective to engage in actions whereby individuals broke into the drilling sites and locked themselves to the drilling equipment. This could delay work for a few hours while those "locked on" were cut from the machinery.

This tactic had been raised before in the campaign, but was seen as unnecessary while the strategy of picketing was proving effective. When our pickets began being overwhelmed by the enormous police presence, people were keen to discuss new strategies that could hinder the test work being done. After all, the enthusiasm that had developed in the campaign was based on its effectiveness in actually impacting the project, not simply protesting against it.

Throughout the history of social movements and community campaigns, acts of individual defiance have at times been inspiring, at other times demobilising. It is important to consider how such individual action will impact upon a campaign and its momentum. When the form of protest is an individual action it can send a message out that people need not get involved because a select group of activists are taking care of things. Those outside of this group become spectators, rather than agents of change.

For the Socialist Party, we had seen how people's understanding of their own role as active opponents the East-West toll road had developed over time. People who had never considered themselves activists before were now standing up to the force of the police and arrogance of government and big business every morning on the picket line. This shift in consciousness – and an understanding of our collective strength – would be absolutely crucial to the success of the campaign. While the transformation so far had been inspiring, it needed to spread further and become stronger.

The danger in conceding to a wholesale shift towards individual "lock ons" was to lose the momentum towards mass collective action – the type of action that had so far put the government on the back foot. One of the strengths of the campaign was that there was mass underlying opposition to the East-West toll road. These people were our goldmine that we needed to draw out onto the streets. The last thing we wanted to do was give them the impression that we had things sorted and didn't need them to get involved.

However, a tactical use of individual "lock ons" and small group occupations of drilling sites, combined with a picket surrounding and protecting these positions, could work to maximise our disruption of the work while demonstrating the importance and method of collective action.

This approach proved effective on October 9. On this day the Linking Melbourne Authority had two drills set up in Carlton North, one on Station Street and the other just around the corner on Davis Street. We had a number of battles to delay the works on

Station Street but ultimately we were outnumbered by the huge police presence there. Never content to give up without fight, we had a quick (and quiet) street meeting where I proposed that we, without warning, collectively run to the other drilling site and set up our picket there, where only a few police officers were currently on guard.

We caught the police by surprise and managed to set up a strong picket at the Davis Street site. Such was the excitement that one of the sections of fence was pushed from its base and several people squeezed in to occupy the drilling site. Before the police could respond experienced picketer Tony Murphy climbed on top of the drill and locked himself on with a sturdy bike lock. While letting the workers out of the now occupied drilling site, we maintained a picket around the fence to stop the police getting in to drag out the occupiers and cut Tony down.

We were now in a strong position and refused to move. We relayed to the police that the only way we would leave the site was if all drilling (including at the other site) would cease for the day. This demand was initially laughed off by the police inspector in charge. A few hours later, after seeing that we weren't budging, it became the basis of negotiation. In the end, the Linking Melbourne Authority conceded and agreed to stop all drilling for the day.

After this victory we had expected the battle to resume again the next day but in a surprise move, the government announced an end to the test drilling with several sites yet to be drilled. The Linking Melbourne Authority attempted to spin the announcement as a positive, claiming all the soil samples needed had been obtained. This was clearly not the case.

With cars, our caravan and picketers blockading the rest of the drilling sites, each day would present new problems for the Linking Melbourne Authority, their drilling contractors

BATTLE BEGINS TO HEAT UP 47

Picketer Tony Murphy locked on to a drill rig while others occupy the drill site. Image: Anthony Main

and the police. We had made the process so difficult and time consuming that the government decided to back away, stopping the preliminary works and ending our need to picket. This was a strategic - and what we would soon understand to be a short-lived - retreat.

While we could claim victory in this phase of the campaign, we knew the government would come back with a new strategy. So we also began preparing plans to regroup and rally our supporters for the next phase of the campaign.

Placard by Mel Gregson

BILLION$ WASTED ON NAPTHINE'S TUNNEL VISION

Socialist Party australia.org
FOR STRUGGLE, SOLIDARITY & SOCIALISM

CHAPTER 4
TARGETING THE PROFITEERS

We called a demonstration at the campaign HQ on Westgarth Street in Fitzroy (the site of our caravan blockade) on Saturday October 13. Despite the terrible weather 500 people turned up. The rain could not dampen people's excitement after we had forced the government to back down. People were keen to find out what it meant and what was next in store.

For the Socialist Party, the rally was not simply an opportunity to celebrate what we had achieved so far. We wanted to use the opportunity to bring everybody onto the same page and propose a new strategy for the campaign.

You would think that by now no one could ignore the role the community picket had played in shaping the dispute, impacting on the project schedule and drawing in public support. But for many, both involved and watching, the political processes were not yet perfectly clear. Frustratingly, some saw the suspension of drilling as an opportunity to revert back to lobbying. Others saw it as an opportunity to join a popular campaign without having to do the hard work of picketing, and proposed that all our effort should go into rallying on the weekends. Both approaches ignored all the lessons learnt through the community picket.

As an alternative, the Socialist Party proposed to move forward on our strengths. It was direct action, we argued, that had forced the government to retreat. From that we should take confidence.

50   BEATING THE BIG END OF TOWN

October 13, 2013 rally against the East-West toll road on Westgarth Street, Fitzroy. Image: Chris Starr

But test drilling was not the only work being conducted on the East-West toll road. The huge construction firms were busy preparing their bids for the lucrative contract to build the road. They, we suggested, were equally valid targets for our community picket as the drilling contractors had been.

After all, the tiny firms involved in the preliminary works were not the main ones driving the project. The big players, the multi-billion dollar construction firms with friends in all the right places, were the ones attempting to rort Victorians out of decades' worth of transport infrastructure funding. Like most multinational corporations, they do their damage from behind closed doors.

The two main construction firms leading the consortia bidding for the contact were Leighton Holdings and Lend Lease. Contracts had not yet been signed, so the East-West toll road remained a dispute between the government and community. But we wanted to make it clear to these profiteers that that this project would be a nightmare that they did not want to get themselves involved in. What better way to make this message clear than to picket their headquarters while they prepare their bids?

For the Socialist Party, we considered this strategy a clear escalation and expected there to be debate around the issue.

However, none of the other political forces made any substantive suggestions about what to do next. To our delight the rally voted unanimously in support of targeting the construction companies that were bidding for the contracts.

RAISING PEOPLE'S SIGHTS

The process towards increasingly radical political action at each stage of the campaign was not a product of luck or wishful thinking. It was the result of a conscious method of organising.

No community campaigner or political aspirant can effect real social change without bringing others with them. For socialists, it's crucial we are able to bring people with us as active, conscious participants. This means convincing people of a certain political perspective, and flowing from that a campaign strategy, in order to organise a movement to effect change.

This would be much easier if everyone agreed that the economic system of capitalism - whereby the levers of the economy and the ability to produce wealth lay in hands of a tiny minority pursuing their own interests – is a rotten way to run the world.

This is what I believe and it's why I'm a socialist, why I study Marxism and why I joined the Socialist Party. But I understand that not everybody looks at world the way that we in the Socialist Party do. Not everybody draws a link between everyday experiences and the way the system functions.

However, what people are very sensitive to are the injustices that capitalism breeds, - especially when they are close to home. It's this fact that makes social change – and socialism – possible.

Every instance where anger or frustration at these injustices is felt or expressed and can be collectivised is an opportunity to effect change. It doesn't always materialise, as campaigns and

52 BEATING THE BIG END OF TOWN

movements need to be consciously built with political ideas and experience. But each represents a possibility to change the world.

For the Socialist Party, each opportunity to help organise people into a community campaign or political movement for change is an opportunity to raise their sights to larger, systemic injustices created by capitalism. The process of political action is itself an eye-opener to the way society functions. Through seeking solutions to local problems, people quickly find the source of their problems run far deeper and spread much further than they had first realised. This realisation can be demoralising in its enormity or intriguing in its complexity. Alongside a guiding theoretical analysis, it can help people better understand the political and economic system we live under and how to alter it.

If the Socialist Party had begun campaigning against the East-West toll road with a lecture about how capitalism works and the need for a worldwide workers' revolution, we would have ended up speaking only to ourselves. Instead we recognised the anger and frustration people felt towards the proposed toll road and discussed this with them. From here we could build a picture of their political consciousness and help raise their sights about what action to take.

At the very beginning we pointed out that due to both major political parties supporting the toll road, only a campaign of mass community action could stop the project. Very few agreed with us, so we encouraged those who did not share our view to test out other approaches. We joined them in this. It actually took years of patient campaigning alongside people employing strategies we knew would be insufficient (always trying to explain why in the process), in order for people to draw the necessary conclusions to take the type of action required to win the campaign.

It remained this way throughout the entire dispute. While always trying to explain the bigger picture and what action would

TARGETING THE PROFITEERS 53

Socialist Party Councillor Stephen Jolly makes the case for targeting the construction firms. Image: Chris Starr

be necessary, we proposed actions and strategies we thought we could convince a majority of at any given time and place, in order to progress the campaign and raise people's political consciousness. Sometimes we would have liked things to move more quickly or action to be more decisive, but bringing people with us at a pace that helped them fully participate was always crucial.

It is this "transitional" method that the Socialist Party employs to make our ideas and theories relevant to building political movements in today's world. In this sense, the campaign to stop the East-West toll road was neither the beginning or the end, but part of the process, of our broader goal of social change.

Unfortunately, not all socialist groups agree with this approach. Some see community campaigns and political movements not as processes to foster and develop, but as opportunities to siphon and recruit. One of Melbourne's student-based socialist groups, Socialist Alternative, routinely takes this approach. This group only got involved in the campaign after we had been getting media coverage. The group's members uniformly ignored the actual tasks facing the campaign, instead choosing to spend their time trying to convince people to come to meetings about topics unrelated to the East-West toll road. They would continue with this until people would have to actively ask them to stop talking to them.

Not having much success with this approach, some then volunteered to take on tasks, none of which were ever done. Some began to claim that their group had led the campaign against the East-West toll road from the beginning, despite having never participated. This approach works for them in their goal of finding one or two people in a crowd of hundreds that may join their group, alienating dozens more in the process. Focusing all their energy on recruitment is how they build their organisation and grow. But it's an approach that hinders the development of community campaigns and political movements, and has led many students to view socialists as wreckers and parasites.

The other socialist group involved in the campaign was the Socialist Alliance, formerly the largest socialist group in Melbourne, but now much smaller. They employed a different strategy, particularly focused on a council-orientated approach in the municipality of Moreland. The Socialist Alliance got involved late in the campaign and because they were not very involved in the direct action, they often argued that decisions should be made in committee meetings, not on the picket line. We disagreed on this as it would have weakened the campaign by taking the decision making out of the hands of those participating in the struggle and developing their political consciousness in the process.

For those interested in socialist ideas, it must be understood that the application of an idea is just as important as the explanation, especially if you want your efforts to actually effect social change. How the different socialist groups work in practice was demonstrated in this campaign.

TARGETING THE PROFITEERS 55

It should never be underestimated how much people can learn about politics on the basis of their own experience. In trying to change things we all come up against limits. Socialist theory can help facilitate this process by bringing the experience of past and distant struggles to the present and by helping to bridge the gap between our current situation and what is required to effect change.

The most important task in political organising is understanding the consciousness and perspectives of the people you are engaging with. It serves no one to wish a different consciousness on people. We must always start from where people are at, then propose a way forward in a transitional way. It was this approach that the Socialist Party was employing when we proposed the campaign target the headquarters of the construction firms with our community picket. This phase of the campaign saw some of the most militant protest actions Melbourne had seen for years, including shutting down the offices of a number of mega corporations.

Picketing an enterence to John Holland, one of the firms bidding for the toll road contract. Image: Brune Goguillon

56   BEATING THE BIG END OF TOWN

GOVERNMENT CRACK DOWN

After building support for picketing the construction firms, we went and did it. Just like the drilling companies, the construction firm John Holland (a subsidiary of Leighton Holdings) thought they could wait us out. For a few days we shut down their offices completely. On later attempts the police secured the premised and kept it open.

Things escalated when we moved on to the other major construction firm, Lend Lease. Their office occupied the top floors of a Docklands office building. One morning we arrived before office hours and blockaded all of the entrances of the building. By about 8.00am dozens of staff were milling around on the footpath, unable to get into the building. Some of them told us they worked for Fujitsu, the company that shared the building with Lend Lease.

Some of these people began talking to the media present and had the potential to distract from the focus on Lend Lease and its plans to profiteer from the toll road project.

The key to running a strong picket line is to make sure it is disciplined and everyone understands their role. If the line were

Picketing Lend Lease, one of the firms bidding for the toll road contract. Image: Sue Jackson

broken every time someone claimed to have a legitimate reason to get through, the whole thing would quickly fall apart. When in control of an entrance or strategic point, it's important to maintain that control. If we were going to let in the Fujitsu staff, it needed to be done in an organised way that did not undermine our ability to shut down Lend Lease.

The Fujitsu employees had company IDs that allowed them to work the lift in the building, most wearing them as lanyards. It was clear that many of the people trying to get in did not work for Lend Lease, however we wanted to be sure no Lend Lease staff sneaked in claiming to work for another company. Socialist Party organiser Mel Gregson negotiated with Peter Ward, the police inspector in charge, that if those claiming to work for Fujitsu lined up at one entrance and showed her their company ID, then they would be let in. He agreed to this proposal. Every fifteen minutes Mel, with the police inspector alongside, spoke to the staff who had arrived, explained what was happening and asked them to line up and have their company ID ready. The rest of us maintained the picket.

All of the news coverage that day featured footage of Mel checking IDs at the entrance, and thanking people for their patience and understanding as they entered one by one through a controlled gap in the picket.

It was incredible that the police had conceded this to us. Even Mel, who proposed and arranged the deal, couldn't believe Ward had agreed to it. The effect was to legitimise our presence and boost the confidence of our picketers who now felt in control of the space.

By that afternoon, right-wing media commentators had gone off their heads, berating the police for allowing us such blatant control of the building. Such was the pressure on Ward, he began lying in the media claiming no arrangement had been made. This was clearly contradicted by the footage, but he was responding to calls from government politicians, shock jocks and other right-wing commentators to arrest and jail us, and to no longer compromise with us.

It's impossible for us to know exactly what was discussed behind closed doors between government ministers and senior police officers. But what was clear to us was that the government saw our targeting of the major construction firms as a step too far. Where there had previously been a reluctance to wage a full-scale assault on our picket, now politicians and media commentators were calling for a crackdown.

In the weeks to follow the police operation was significantly stepped up. A new task force was set up to deal with the East-West related pickets. What this taskforce actually consisted of was never clear, but it helped give the impression that we were criminals who needed to be policed. In effect, it amounted to more aggressive policing tactics, including the violent targeting of women protesters who were seen to be leading the campaign.

At the same time the state government announced plans to introduce new laws to increase police powers. The focus of the changes was to make it easier for the police to "move-on" protesters even if no offense had been committed. There was no hiding the fact that the laws were aimed squarely at our campaign against the East-West toll road, though could also have serious consequences for trade unions engaging in industrial action and protests more generally.

In December 2013 the government tabled these changes to the Summary Offences Act. When speaking in favour of the bill in parliament Liberal MP Ken Smith indicated who wanted the new laws to be used against: "I am talking about one of the protesters who has forced the introduction of this legislation. I am talking about people like Anthony Main. He is 37 years old. He hates

TARGETING THE PROFITEERS 59

Picketing the Linking Melbourne Authority office. Image: Brune Goguillon

right-wing politicians, he hates big business and he has said he is proud to be a pest. I will tell you what: when this legislation goes through, let us see how proud he is when he gets dragged up by the coppers. Let us see how proud he will be then, with his mate Cr Stephen Jolly and Yarra City Council."

The Liberals were furious that our pickets and protests were having an effect. This in itself was a boost to our campaign. However, we were now provoking a serious response that could have effects beyond the East-West toll road.

The changes to the laws gave the police more power to "move-on" a person or group and to ban them from an area for 24-hours. If a person or group was given a "move-on order" three times within a six month period then the police could apply for an "exclusion order" which banned them from a given area for up to a year. The contravention of these orders carried a maximum penalty of two years in jail.

In the media, politicians and the police were adamant that these new powers would be used against us at the first available opportunity. When people grew concerned, we tried to reinforce the bigger picture: it is through mass picketing that we can stop the East-West toll road from being built, and it is through mass resistance that we can make these laws inoperable. The new powers were primarily a deterrent, as the logistics of arresting everyone at a sizable protest would be problematic to implement. This is especially the case if the protest had public support and could draw in greater numbers in response.

We argued that this was another turning point in the campaign at which we needed to focus again on building our numbers and increasing our support base. If they did start "moving on" and arresting picketers we needed greater numbers to take their place. This was our strategy to make the laws irrelevant. In the end, despite having these laws on the books the police never felt confident to use them against us.

XMAS RALLY FOR PUBLIC TRANSPORT

Back in outreach mode, we used the final weeks of 2013 to build for an end of year Xmas rally. It was important to register everything we had achieved before people wind down over the summer break. On December 15 we held another rally at Smith Reserve in Fitzroy with the theme "All I want for Xmas is better public transport". Around 500 people turned out.

The goal at this juncture was to further consolidate our inner-city support base, but to also outline a strategy to win more support for our campaign in the outer suburbs and regional areas. We invited other pro-public transport, community and environment groups to rally alongside us. We were especially focused on winning support for the idea that the billions of dollars that would be wasted on the East-West toll road would be better spent on improving public transport across Victoria.

The Socialist Party proposed the idea that we take the campaign caravan out on a tour of Victoria and speak to people directly. We felt that if we were able to discuss the issues relating to the East-West toll road with people face to face about how this would affect them and their communities we could broaden our support base across the state. This tour would then culminate in a central rally in Melbourne in the lead up to the Victorian state election. By doing the groundwork to build a strong rally we could bring the issue of the East-West toll road and public transport to the fore of the election campaign.

Still some others in the broader campaign had failed to acknowledge the role of the community pickets in leading the opposition to the East-West toll road. This was evident in some of the speeches at the rally. Some argued that we needed to embark on a (implicitly pro-Labor) marginal seats electoral campaign. Others argued that we should raise tens of thousands of dollars to hire lawyers to negotiate with the government. The Greens, if nothing but consistent, asked everyone to vote for them come the election in twelve months' time.

Diversity in ideas and tactics can be beneficial to a campaign, so long as these ideas are working towards the same goal. Unfortunately, these speeches did not reinforce the idea of ordinary people effecting change through collective action; they all wanted to outsource the job to someone else. This stemmed, in most cases, from a lack of confidence in building mass support for the campaign and a lack of political strategy of how to do it.

Thankfully the best response from those at the Xmas rally was for the Socialist Party's outward approach. Hundreds of people at the rally signed up to get involved in the direct action campaign and the caravan tour. We ended the rally with a few drinks at a local pub, celebrating how far we had come and looked forward to a well-earned break over summer. Unfortunately we would have no such luck. The very next day we were dragged back out onto the streets.

62   BEATING THE BIG END OF TOWN

Poster by Mel Gregson

NO EAST-WEST TUNNEL
TRAINS, NOT TOLLS!

All I want for xmas is

BETTER PUBLIC TRANSPORT

DON'T LET NAPHINE WASTE $8 BILLION ON A TOLL ROAD TUNNEL WHEN WE DESPERATELY NEED INVESTMENT IN PUBLIC TRANSPORT!

COME AND JOIN WITH OTHERS CAMPAIGNING FOR REAL SOLUTIONS TO MELBOURNE'S TRANSPORT WOES

This rally is organised by various community and residents groups opposed to the East West Link. For more info contact Mel on 0400 588 202

COMMUNITY RALLY
SUNDAY 15 DECEMBER
1pm @ Smith Reserve on Alexandra Parade
(next to Fitzroy Pool)
Family friendly event

CHAPTER 5
DIRECT ACTION TURNS SITUATION

At about 5.00am on Monday December 16 we received a flood of messages to our campaign phone reporting a major police operation in Fitzroy and Collingwood. Residents awoke to the sound of a police helicopter flying overhead while hundreds of police officers assisted Linking Melbourne Authority staff to set up four new drill sites. This dead-of-the-night operation occurred despite the government's assurance that the test drilling had finished.

This totally ended any pretence of community consultation in relation to work on the East-West toll road. The Napthine Government had believed it could deal with opposition to the project through the tried-and-true method of fake "consultation". The government and Linking Melbourne Authority had encouraged opponents of the project to submit detailed submissions to its Comprehensive Impact Statement (CIS) Assessment Committee.

Unfortunately some involved in the campaign took this process at face value and believed that they could influence the Assessment Committee by producing lengthy, well prepared and professional documents detailing why the East-West toll road was a dud project.

Even the very best of these submissions would be completely ignored. The whole process was a "Potemkin Village" constructed to divert opponents of the East-West toll road down an avenue in which they held no power or authority. This is because the Assessment Committee itself held no real power or authority.

An example of the rubber-stamping expected of committees such as these was seen in late 2013 with the advisory committee that was set up to look at transport matters. This committee was handpicked by Planning Minister Matthew Guy and was expected to promote the East-West toll road as Victoria's central and premier transport project. When five of the six committee members disagreed, they were left with little choice but to resign. The chair of the committee later said of the East-West toll road: "It is not smart, innovative or progressive thinking" and "it is fraught with problems as well as showing a short-sighted and politically expedient approach".

Had this committee held any real power in shaping government policy it would have ditched the East-West toll road in favour of public transport. That is what the "experts" on the committee agreed on. Unfortunately, that's not how this system works, so they resigned and the government found new "experts" who would happily manufacture a justification for its transport policies.

These incredibly wasteful and seemingly pointless fake "consultations" actually do serve an important purpose from the government's point of view. After the long, expensive and time-consuming process of making submissions that lead nowhere, most opponents then give up, tired and demoralised. It is the perfect way for governments to misdirect a community's energy and resources.

It is for these reasons the Socialist Party did not encourage people to make submissions to the CIS Assessment Committee. Instead of trying to convince powerless bureaucrats we called on people to focus their energy on convincing ordinary people to join the community pickets. This is where a real impact could be had.

Had more people put all their time and energy into community campaigning, rather than fake government consultation, we may have stopped the East-West toll road earlier than we did. This is a lesson for the future.

FITZROY UNDER SIEGE

The recommencing of drilling through an almost military-like operation in the middle of the night jolted the community picket back into action. Though we didn't race out of the gates as swiftly as one might hope.

The sheer scale of the police operation was shocking. Without warning streets had been closed off and residents' cars impounded. Locals were stopped and questioned for simply walking down the street. More than a hundred police swarmed residential streets, very much alert and on edge.

One Collingwood resident was fined by police for asking why they had set up a fence only metres from her front door. They yelled at her to go back inside. When she refused, police officers then followed her to her car, handing her two more infringement notices while she sat in the driver's seat. She maintained that all she had done was ask questions and that the police were immediately suspicious and aggressive toward her. We heard many other stories like this.

It was clear that the police felt as though they had entered enemy territory. In some respects our campaign resembled an unarmed guerrilla rebellion. Our main strength and advantage was our deep roots in the local community. This led the police to overreact, further alienating local residents, pushing them closer towards us and our campaign.

By early morning we had sent out a text message to our campaign list calling people to an emergency meeting at the campaign HQ. By the time we convened the meeting of about thirty people, there were hundreds of police on the streets protecting the four new drilling sites. The cocky attitudes of the Linking Melbourne Authority supervisors and the police had angered us, but we weren't immediately sure what to do.

It was clear by this stage that we were drastically outnumbered and ill-prepared. At the height of the community picket we had built up momentum and a routine that people were familiar with. On this day we had not been afforded the luxury of preparation time. Clearly this was part of the Government's new tactic. With only a few dozen picketers and hundreds of police there was no way that we could have any impact on the drilling now underway at four separate sites - but we didn't want to go home defeated.

It would have been a demoralising experience to simply protest at one of the new drill sites without impacting on the work. Instead, the Socialist Party proposed that we escalate our disruption tactics by occupying the road through a sit down protest on busy Brunswick Street.

So far throughout the campaign we had been conscious of putting forward concrete strategies, like pickets and occupations, that could actually impact on the preliminary works. This had served us very well, helping us convince people who did not consider themselves militant enough to take radical action like defying police orders and shutting down the offices of multinational companies.

To now revert to the more symbolic protest action of a road sit down seemed like a step backwards. In some ways it was. We argued that our options were to admit defeat on this day and try to mobilise for tomorrow, or to show the Government that we would not be outmanoeuvred by them. Most people were willing to give it a go, though a few argued that it would upset people too much.

For most people who have attended a rally or march,

DIRECT ACTION TURNS SITUATION 67

Road occupation on Brunswick Street, Fitzroy. Image: Brune Goguillon

occupying a road and causing disruption to a city is part and parcel of protesting. However, in a political climate where protest movements, community organising and industrial action are at an all-time ebb, going against the status quo can be confronting. This is reinforced by the fact that many protests that occur are disconnected from any real strategy to achieve their aims and goals, and are seen by many as a waste of time. This perception is not helped by some protesters who prefer to revel in their own feelings of self-importance rather than focus on what their actions and tactics are actually achieving.

In this case we couldn't effectively disrupt drilling, but we could cause some disruption to the heavy-handed control the police had established over our community. After all, whatever disruption we caused today would pale in comparison to the disruption caused if the East-West toll road was built. So we agreed, after much discussion, to occupy the road in a sit down protest.

It was clear that this tactic, under these conditions, would likely result in arrest. To keep things interesting, we agreed that we would sit down for as long as possible, then as soon as the police

68   BEATING THE BIG END OF TOWN

Protesters moments prior to be chased down and arrested by police. Image: Stephanie Jane

moved in to arrest us we would collectively stand up and move off the road. Our intention was to then regroup to occupy another section of road, keeping the action going for as long as possible.

We sat down and blocked Brunswick Street for about half an hour. It was peak hour and we caused major disruptions. While some motorists were unhappy with us, many others expressed their support for our campaign. At least one person caught up in the traffic decided to join us.

The police were furious. After unsuccessful negotiations the officer-in-charge called in the Public Order Response Team (PORT) to drag us off the road and arrest us. Much to the entertainment of onlookers, as the police marched toward us in formation, we waited until the last second to collectively jump up and leave the road. From here we marched down a few side streets to lose the police, then again occupied the road – this time the very busy Alexandra Parade.

Again, we waited until the police arrived and were ready to remove us, then jumped up and marched away. By the third time the police had had enough. On our third attempt the police chased us down the road and arrested four protesters. It was clear the officers had been instructed who to arrest, and they later admitted to have targeted those who they believed were ringleaders.

Those who were arrested were told that they would be charged by summons for obstructing a road. This was a relatively minor charge and did nothing to deter us. After being manhandled, all were let go. We then held a meeting to discuss our plans for the next day.

While the brief road occupations had lifted spirits and garnered us media attention to expose how the government had gone back on its word to recommence test drilling, we now needed to seriously assess how we would approach the four new drilling sites.

The Socialist Party put forward the idea of calling an ongoing occupation of one of the central drilling sites. If we could build up a round-the-clock presence at one of the sites we could recreate momentum and give ourselves the best chance to happen upon a weakness to exploit.

We believed that a 24/7 community picket would be required if the project ever made it to the construction phase, so introducing the idea now could help prepare for that. While almost everyone at the meeting agreed, when it was time to decide who would stay overnight, everyone looked down at their shoes. Only two people of the two dozen present could commit to it. It is one thing to recognise what strategy and tactics can move a campaign forward but you also need to be able to carry it out with the forces you have, not the forces you'd like to have.

Unable to execute an ongoing occupation we agreed to use the rest of the afternoon to build for a mass picket the next morning. We agreed to use all of our forces to try and shut down one of the drilling sites.

Picketing the drilling site on Westgarth St as Rosie sits on top of the drill rig. Image: Oliver Marras

THE BATTLE OF WESTGARTH STREET

The major police operation employed to recommence drilling, coupled with the dishonesty and bullying tactics employed by police and the Linking Melbourne Authority, enraged many residents who up until this point had not been active in the campaign. Also, while the road occupations had negligible impact on the drilling, the coverage of our protest on the news was extensive. These events ended up strengthening our campaign, rather than overwhelming us.

The following day we had our largest turnout to the picket, with many new faces coming for the first time. By early morning we had at least a hundred picketers involved. The news teams had also arrived to see what would happen next.

We had spent the previous afternoon and evening organising people to meet at the Westgarth Street site with the plan of using all of our forces to attempt to stop the drill that was located on the corner of busy Brunswick Street. On my routine check of all the drill sites before dawn, I realised that a couple of people had decided to break into two of the other sites overnight and lock themselves to the drill rigs.

In contrast to the open and democratic way that we had been organising they had decided to do this without consulting others in the campaign. This was disappointing. Not only did it risk derailing a plan that was democratically agreed the previous day, but this type of secret organising does not build the trust required to shape an effective campaign. Far from empowering people it makes people feel disenfranchised by imposing unilateral decisions without accountability.

With people soon to gather at the other site we planned to target, those locked to the other two drills were left with a couple of people to keep watch. Without a picket present, those locked to the drills were easily removed by the police after a couple of hours.

The most important task was to re-establish the community picket and focus on building collective action. First we used cars to block entry to the drilling site. Then, with almost a hundred people arriving by dawn, we established our community picket around the drilling site. The police were aggressive but our picketers were angry and determined. As the police created a commotion, pushing and trying to drag people away, one of the picketers snuck inside the site and scaled the drill rig.

Rosie Elliott, a 60 year old resident of North Fitzroy, climbed up the machinery and perched herself on top of the rig. Our picketers quickly encircled the drilling site, linking arms to stop police from dragging her down. The cockiness of the police and the Linking Melbourne Authority from the previous day immediately gave way to frustration and despair. The media reported the events as a win for us and an embarrassment for the government. Despite the huge police operation we had still managed to impact on the drilling with more people than ever on the picket and a 60 year old resident showing resolute determination. It was inspiring to those watching on the news. We held strong on Westgarth Street and managed to stop works there for the rest of the day.

The next day we arrived to an even larger police presence. After the previous day's win more people had come to the picket but we were still outnumbered. Hundreds of police were lined up shoulder to shoulder around the drill site that we had shut down the previous day. Again, it was unclear if we were going to be able to impact the drilling.

Just before convening the morning meeting to propose a plan, I noticed that while all of the police were guarding the drill site they had left the water supply they were using unattended about fifty metres down the road. If we could disrupt the water supply to the drill rig, it would disrupt the drilling.

We quickly convened a meeting of picketers across the road. There were again some new faces, but we didn't have much time to go into detail. I explained that we had an opportunity to disrupt the drilling by cutting off their water supply, but only if we moved immediately and quickly.

With everyone in tow we acted as if we were marching to the fence of the drilling site but at the last second ran to surround the water supply in the middle of Westgarth Street. A few police officers tried in vain to defend it but we had caught them by surprise. We formed a large huddle around the water supply and shut it off.

This manoeuvre was to the delight of the TV crews present, who were out in force that day. Again, they broadcast footage of the determined community defying police and embarrassing the government.

Eventually the drilling company found a new water supply and this time ensured it was well protected by police. Some of the police from the other drilling sites had been diverted for this. The site at the other end of Westgarth Street was now only being guarded by a handful of cops. By this stage we had close to 150 picketers present.

DIRECT ACTION TURNS SITUATION 73

I got on the megaphone and suggested that we all march, very quickly, to the other drilling site. The picketers did not need much encouragement and within seconds the entire 150-strong crowd was running down Westgarth Street with dozens of police officers and TV cameras trailing.

When we arrived the few police protecting the site were totally overwhelmed. Immediately the fences came down. Some picketers entered the site while others dragged the fence down the street. One of our picketers hit the emergency stop button on the drill so others could climb up it. Once again we had outmanoeuvred the police and the Linking Melbourne Authority.

After the huge police operation to set up four new drilling sites, we had now managed to stop work two days in a row. The government was starting to look very foolish. That day the *Herald Sun* reported that so far $300,000 had been spent on the police operation, dubbed "Operation Burrow". By the end of the dispute the *Herald Sun* claimed that more than $5 million had been spent combating the pickets. They quoted one figure from police sources claiming that $4.3 million was spent on extra police shifts and overtime costs. They also said another $220,000 was spent on private

Community picket on Westgarth St in Fitzroy. Image: Mel Gregson

74 BEATING THE BIG END OF TOWN

security and $400,000 was spent by the Linking Melbourne Authority on extra equipment and overtime costs. These figures highlight how effective the direct action was.

While some in the media attempted to blame us for the blowout cost, it wasn't difficult to point out that this was small change compared to the billions of dollars the government was willing to waste on a socially, economically and environmentally disastrous project. If they stopped the project, all of that money could be put to better use. Aside from outlandish claims that they would "make [us] pay", the government and their lackeys in the mainstream press had no answer to this.

A GOVERNMENT OVERREACHING

By setting up four drill rigs at once, backed up by a huge police presence, the government thought it could overwhelm our campaign. What they hadn't reckoned with was the fact that our pickets were mobile and fast moving, and we were gaining support. In fact, the more they brutalised us in front of TV cameras, the more people joined in the next day. Their tactic to get the drilling back on schedule had not worked. After the battle of Westgarth Street they never returned to setting up four sites at once again. This meant the preliminary works would take even longer to complete.

The drilling stopped over the Christmas and New Year period and our campaign entered 2014 feeling more confident than ever that we could win!

On January 8, 2014 the government announced plans to restart the drilling on a further fourteen sites. Far from being close to finishing as had previously been stated, the Linking Melbourne Authority now claimed that the contractors bidding for the project had in fact requested even more soil samples. It seemed we would be picketing through the rest of summer.

DIRECT ACTION TURNS SITUATION 75

A pre-dawn community picket on Alexandra Parade. Image: Mel Gregson

The police were constantly shocked about our ability to mobilise people quickly and in the most difficult of circumstances. On January 9, Melbourne was in the middle of a heatwave with temperatures hovering around 40 degrees celsius. That afternoon local residents alerted us to an unexplained police presence on Charlotte Street in Collingwood. We sent out a text to our rapid response team and within twenty minutes forty people were there ready to picket despite the blazing afternoon sun. Locals brought us cold drinks, icy poles and ice packs to stay cool while we stopped the new drill site from being set up.

The police responded to the success of our flying pickets by setting up a semi-permanent police station on the grassy strip in the middle of Alexandra Parade. While this gave them a convenient home base for their daily operation, it also meant that the thousands of motorists passing each hour saw the enormous police resources being wasted on this project.

Under pressure to get results, the police began using more openly brutal tactics. They used significant force even against teenagers and elderly people. The Public Order Response Team (PORT) was particularly despised after consistently targeting women picketers, sometimes using tactics that amounted to sexual assault. While some police officers revelled in any opportunity to inflict pain on picketers, most were clearly frustrated to be there.

During quiet times on the picket we often discussed with police what our campaign was about and what we were trying to achieve. Some listened more than others. Some said they agreed with us. At rough times, when the police were using force against us, we would remind them whose interests they were defending, and that if the road was to be built it would be their fault. We take this approach not because we have romantic illusions that the police may switch sides and support us but in order to take advantage of the contradictions that exist.

If you ask most people what function police play in society, most would say they exist to enforce the law. This is generally true, but police do not enforce the law equally. This is demonstrated by the fact that as of January 2014, not a single charge had been laid against any of our picketers. By the end of the campaign only a few dozen very minor charges had been laid, with many being dismissed in court. Yet thousands of police hours and millions of dollars were spent trying to stop our campaign.

Some people first came to the picket thinking that the police would treat us fairly if we were polite to them. It didn't take long until they understood whose side the police were on. Others came to the pickets as spectators, wanting to support the campaign but considering themselves "non-violent". This is a nice concept, but when people are being brutalised simply for standing up for their community, their city and the environment, the idea that we can choose to avoid violence becomes farcical. Most of these people ended up joined the picket after they saw what was actually going on.

The fact that we managed to maintain a very disciplined and organised picket made it much harder for the police to paint us as the aggressors. This discipline was mainly achieved through having clear objectives. We all knew what we were trying to achieve at any given

DIRECT ACTION TURNS SITUATION   77

time, so it was easy to remain united in those goals.

To achieve the same type of discipline in the police force, and to convince officers with kids and grandparents to brutalise teenagers and elderly people, it helps if they believe that what they are doing is right or necessary. Before being enlisted in "Operation Burrow" officers were given briefings about who we were and what to expect. They were told outlandish and ridiculous stories about us in order to diminish any sympathy they may have had for our cause. Officers were rotated regularly so as to not build familiarity with us. That such tactics needed to be employed demonstrated a weakness. If the goal of senior police is to demonise and dehumanise us in the eyes of officers in order to make it easier for them to brutalise us, then clearly we should work against that image, not reinforce it.

It is a similar tactic used by conservative commentators in the mainstream media. By consistently calling us criminals and demanding we be jailed, they hoped to build the perception that we were in the wrong, even if there was no evidence of this. During January, when many in the press take time off, the coverage of campaign became more erratic. Some of the journalists who came to the pickets were new to the profession and were clearly unaware

Police used increasingly aggressive tactics during the dispute. Image: Chris Starr

of what their employers wanted from them. Yet with the media cycle now moving at such a fast pace, some of their articles got put online immediately, then edited later. On many occasions the first version of an article on *The Age* or *Herald Sun* website would be pretty accurate and favourable to us. Throughout the day it would be changed by editors, sometimes up to three or four times, until it consisted only of exaggerations and dramatic falsifications.

On one occasion the *Herald Sun* published a photo with the caption "Anthony Main holds fellow protester Mel Gregson's hair and head as she yells at police". It was actually an image taken the moment Mel had been punched in the face by a police officer. I happened to be standing right behind her when it happened. Luckily, the assault was so blatant that the officer was removed from the police line and did not return. This however didn't stop the mainstream media making up a wholly different sensationalised story that made us look like the aggressors.

Throughout the course of the campaign we suffered a few injuries. Toby Dite's foot was broken after being run over by a police car carrying Premier Denis Napthine. Kat Galea had her head slammed into a parked car by police and was hospitalised. On

Anthony Main speaking to media during a picket on Alexandra Parade.
Image: Sean Bedlam

another occasion the police started a rumour that Mel Gregson was pregnant and soon after she was kicked in the pelvis by an officer. Luckily she was not actually pregnant. I myself was kicked in the head by police a few times at the pickets. Everyone who was a regular on the picket suffered cuts and bruises.

On two occasions we were able to get officers removed from duty because of their conduct, but no further action was ever taken. In fact, protesters who complained of police brutality were routinely threatened with being charged themselves.

TWO MONTHS OF PICKETS

Images of picketers being dragged, punched, thrown and pushed around were broadcast across the country for the next two months. But so were images of us getting back up determined to keep our community campaign strong. Throughout January and February 2014 we picketed drilling every single weekday from 6:30am until the mid afternoon. Often we would be up at 4.00am scouting the drilling sites and making plans for the day.

It was during this period that people began to realise that this was a real struggle that would not end quietly. The amount of attention we drew to problems related to the East-West toll road had a significant impact on public opinion about the project. The government realised that far from wearing us down, our campaign was getting stronger.

In March, after two months of intense struggle, the government finally gave up despite still having several sites left to drill. The Linking Melbourne Authority claimed it had all the soil and rock samples it needed to tender the project. This was proven false in the subsequent months when the consortium led by Leighton Holdings pulled out of the bidding process citing geotechnical risks, most likely due to a lack of data.

80   BEATING THE BIG END OF TOWN

Our direct action had a serious impact on the government's timeline. It also had an important influence on the politics surrounding the project. Everyone was talking about it and forming an opinion about it. As the election neared polls continued to show a majority in favour of investment in public transport over roads. The project that the Liberal government saw as its ticket to re-election was quickly becoming a liability.

NO EAST-WEST TUNNEL COMMUNITY PICKET ACTION ALERT!

5:30am Wednesday January 29

Meet 5:30am at the corner of Queens Parade & Alexandra Parade, Clifton Hill.

The Linking Melbourne Authority is already behind in its drilling schedule. This mounts enormous pressure on the government and puts the whole East West Link project in jeopardy. Help us continue to send the message:

No mandate! No tunnel!

To receive alerts by phone txt 'tunnel' to 0432 447 036

One of our daily 'Action Alerts' for the community picket. Image: Mel Gregson

CHAPTER 6
BUILDING UP POLITICAL PRESSURE

The growing confidence of our campaign encouraged more forces to come out to oppose the East-West toll road. Moreland Council got behind a rally against the project in March 2014. Around 2,000 people marched down Sydney Road protesting against the government's plans. Around the same time a group of high profile lawyers came together to discuss the prospect of launching a Supreme Court challenge against the project. One of the picketers, Tony Murphy, was to be the litigant.

The extra months of community pickets had helped further strengthen our local support. But the need to reach out to people in the outer suburbs and regional areas remained. Our caravan tour had been postponed by the recommencement of drilling the pervious December. It was now time to put it back on the agenda.

CARAVAN TOUR

Everyone agreed that we needed to make the East-West toll road the key issue in the November 2014 state election. However, there wasn't agreement on how to go about doing this.

There was an ingrained tendency amongst many in the campaign to understand an orientation towards the election as a plan to tell people who to vote for. The sad reality in most of Victoria (and most of Australia) is that there is no consistent,

82 BEATING THE BIG END OF TOWN

The campaign caravan visited Geelong during the tour. Image: Kathleen Galea

community based, pro-worker political force that deserves our support. Simply telling people to vote against the current Liberal government wouldn't suffice, as Labor had said they would build the East-West toll road if the contracts were signed prior to the election. Campaigning for the Greens wouldn't achieve much either if both major parties supported the project. Focusing on pro-public transport independents, and standing our own candidates in the name of the campaign, could have been an option if our campaign was larger and had more resources. But that was not possible at this stage.

We needed to find a way to focus people's attention on the East-West toll road without sowing illusions that any of the major parties were going to solve the problem for us. So far we had done this by organising in the community, not by sowing illusions in politicians. In keeping with this approach, we proposed the caravan tour as a way to convince and mobilise people across Victoria to build for a rally based on three demands:

- *Scrap the East-West tunnel*
- *Rip up the contracts*
- *Invest in public transport*

By taking these simple but precise demands out to the far

reaches of Melbourne and Victoria we planned to convince people that organising to force change upon politicians is more powerful than simply voting for them and hoping for the best.

Through engaging people on the street and inviting other pro-public transport groups to join us, we planned for the caravan tour to conclude with a large public rally in the Melbourne CBD on June 28, 2014. This was early enough to influence the election debate, yet far enough away to give us time to do the work required.

Despite some people struggling with the idea of campaigning in the election but not for any particular party, we won general agreement for this plan. Though even then some still pushed for the caravan tour to focus on Liberal/Labor marginal seats.

Far from working to get Labor elected at the next election the task was to continue to heap pressure on them, exposing their fake opposition and attempting to change their position. Instead of visiting marginal seats we needed to visit areas that were crying out for public transport infrastructure. We needed to highlight the big business influence over both the major parties and point towards the need to build a mass movement to win investment in public transport. Over the course of three months we took that message to about a dozen locations and found a great deal of support for what we were saying.

From the beginning of the caravan tour it was clear that the government's pro-East-West toll road propaganda had not soothed people's anger about the lack of transport and services in the outer suburbs. We spoke with isolated young mothers in Mernda, angry students in Belgrave, and fed up workers in Geelong and Ballarat who were forced to travel long distances by car. Frustration about the lack of public transport was consistent across the state and both Labor and the Liberals were ignoring it.

We handed out well over 100,000 leaflets during the caravan

tour and had conversations with thousands of people, while tens of thousands more noticed our presence. While modest in the scheme of a huge state like Victoria, home to over five million people, this outreach work coupled with the publicity we were getting via the mainstream press meant that our message was reaching further than ever before.

RIP UP THE CONTRACTS

The "rip up the contracts" demand proved to be vital as the election neared and as more and more people questioned the merits of the project. Labor had changed their position on the East-West toll road so many times it was difficult to keep up. Their current position, and the one they had planned to take to the election, was one of fake opposition. While wanting to criticise the government over the increasingly unpopular East-West toll road, Labor also wanted to build it! So they said they were against the project, but if contracts were signed before the election the new government's hands would be tied and it would have to go ahead. This position allowed them to pretend that they were opposed to the project and cynically blame the Liberals for it going ahead. They, like everyone, expected the contracts to be signed before the election.

With the Liberals on the nose and Labor slightly ahead in opinion polls the election had become a significant potential turning point. If we were to defeat the project we had to expose Labor's contradictory position and pressure them into committing to rip up any contracts the Liberals signed.

The Socialist Party's distrust of Labor does not come simply from the party's long history of dishonesty and sell-outs. There was a material basis for the Labor Party's support for the East-West toll road. It is true to say that the Liberal Party is the traditional

We collected hundreds of photo petitions during the caravan tour. Image: Mel Gregson

party of big business and the wealthy elite, while the Labor Party was originally set up to provide a political voice for workers. More than a century later, these distinctions are of historical interest but of little consequence today. While they come from different traditions, and have their own peculiarities, for all intents and purposes they both now represent the interests of big business. Both may, at certain times, favour one section of big business over another. But it is wishful thinking to believe Labor would ever put the interests of ordinary people ahead of business. The minor differences that do still exist between the major parties are more about style rather than substance.

Some argue that Labor is a workers' party because of its history. Once upon a time Labor had a very active working class base, and even socialists worked within it. But it has always had a leadership with a pro-capitalist outlook, easily integrated into the establishment whenever the party achieved success. This conflict between the expectation of its working class members and the actual conduct of its leadership when in power greatly influenced

Australian politics throughout the 20th Century.

In the 1980s the actual nature of the Labor Party began to change. A culmination of the struggle to oust socialist trends within its ranks and within the union movement, Labor rejected the "social democracy" of its past and adopted the same neoliberal economic program as the Liberal Party. In order to achieve this, and as a result of this shift, the party began to diminish its democratic structures and lose its working class base. While many trade unions are still affiliated to the party, and workers often still vote for Labor at elections, they do not participate in it actively or organise to influence the party's policies.

An example of how much the Labor Party has changed over time can be seen when comparing the Labor Councillors of the 1970s to those of today. In 1977 the Fitzroy Mayor, Bill Peterson, was famously arrested in his Mayoral robes at a protest against the F-19 Freeway. In the battle against the East-West toll road not a single Labor Party Councillor ever turned up to a picket or risked arrest in defence of the community.

Today Labor takes just as much money from big business as

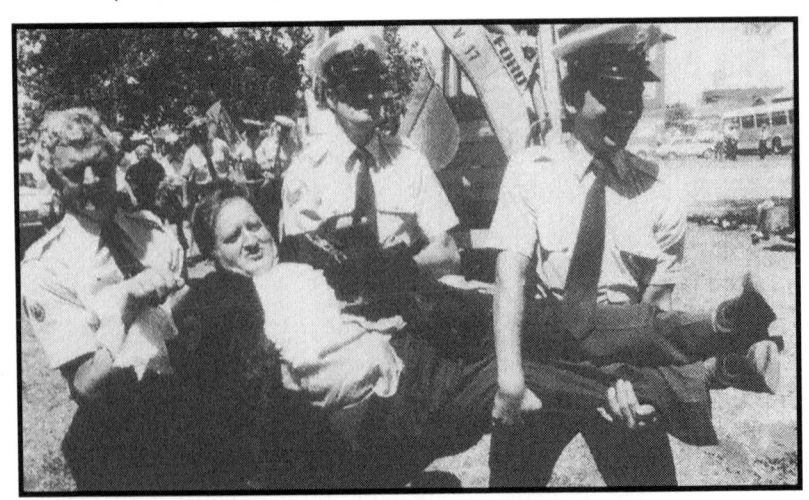

In 1977 Labor Mayor of Fitzroy Bill Peterson was arrested for protesting the F-19 freeway. Image: Fitzroy History Society

the Liberals, including from the oil and road lobby and the big developer and construction firms. These interest groups are just as likely to look to Labor to pursue their interests. Interests like the East-West toll road.

The rightward shift of the Labor Party is also reflected in the trade unions, most of which are formally affiliated to the party. While on some occasions affiliated unions have acted independently (usually under pressure from their membership), in this dispute almost all of them took their cues from Labor and supported the East-West Link.

Some of the more right-wing unions like the Australian Workers Union (AWU), representing civil construction workers, and the Transport Workers Union (TWU), representing truck drivers, openly supported the project on the basis that it would create jobs in the industries where they represented workers.

A couple of other unions like the Rail, Tram and Bus Union (RTBU) and the Electrical Trades Union (ETU), opposed the project as many more jobs would be created for their members by the expansion of public transport. Unfortunately these unions were never very vocal about their opposition or active in the community campaign.

Under the influence of Labor Party politics, most union leaders today are narrowly focused on supporting the expansion of their own specific industry regardless of broader community concerns.

In contrast to this many of the trade union leaders of the past were socialists of one variety or another. This meant that they fought for wages and conditions within the framework of fighting for a different type of society. This led to many unions holding significant weight in society and making huge gains, especially during the 1960s and 1970s. In those times many unions were active in community campaigns around broader social and environmental issues.

88   BEATING THE BIG END OF TOWN

The challenge ahead is to break the influence of Labor within the unions and imbue them with socialist ideas and a community orientation. If we can achieve this, future struggles against projects like the East-West toll road could be led, fought and won by our unions. Fighting trade unions, alongside determined community groups, would be a formidable force to be reckoned with.

THE RALLY AND CHANGING PUBLIC OPINION

In the lead up to the June 28 rally a number of polls and surveys were taken about the East-West Link and public transport. One poll in *The Age* showed that only one in four Victorians thought that the East-West Link should be the government's highest infrastructure priority. Instead most people wanted to see investment in public transport, specifically an expansion of the underground train network.

Around 3,000 people came out to the June 28 rally. The rally was significant as it brought together community groups from right across Melbourne and even from some regional areas. The rally was in reality a culmination of months of outreach work. It was a public expression of the fact that we had managed to turn public opinion. The government recognised that people were now questioning whether the East-West toll road would actually go ahead. Intent on digging a deeper hole, two days after our rally the government formally approved plans for the project. This only reinforced people's feeling that they were being led up the garden path.

With momentum building against the government Yarra Council had been in confidential discussions about the prospect of launching its own legal action against the project. While viewing this as an auxiliary and not the solution, Socialist Party councillor Stephen Jolly supported the idea. Unfortunately the majority of the Labor and Greens councillors did not. Knowing there would be

BUILDING UP POLITICAL PRESSURE 89

3,000 people attended the June 28 rally in the Melbourne CBD. Image: W. van Leeuwen

backlash, these councillors kept this decision under wraps, hiding behind the veil of "confidentiality".

Soon after neighbouring Moreland Council had similar discussions. On that council the Labor councillors were more open to the idea of using legal action to undermine the Liberal government in the lead up to the state election. Moreland Council voted in favour of launching a case in the Supreme Court, a move that thankfully put the councillors at Yarra under pressure to follow suit.

We encouraged people to lobby the Labor and Green councillors at Yarra to support the court action. With the issue now out in the open, and both parties formally claiming to oppose the project, neither wanted to be seen to be dragging their feet. With these pressures upon them they all ended up falling into line and supported the court case.

To keep pressure on the state Labor opposition, we began a series of pickets at the electoral offices of inner-city Labor MPs. Some were so upset about this they begged us to stop as our protests were drawing unwanted attention to the fact that Labor intended to build the East-West toll road.

BEATING THE BIG END OF TOWN

LIBERAL PARTY FUNDRAISER

While we put a lot of heat on Labor at this time, we didn't let the government off the hook. When we heard the Liberals would be holding a fundraiser event to raise money for their state election campaign, we decided to crash it.

The event was held at the swish Regent Plaza Ballroom on Collins Street in the CBD. It was specifically aimed at the corporate elite in and around the transport and construction sectors. For $10,000 a head you could come along and rub shoulders with MPs including Premier Dennis Napthine, Transport Minister Terry Mulder and the Planning Minister Matthew Guy. This was basically an event where the Liberals were getting paid to carry out the dictats of the oil, road and construction lobby while they all drank champagne.

We called for a picket at the event and about a hundred people turned up. We locked arms across the entrance and government figures and their guests could only get through if the police broke our line. Such was the resolve of our people taking a stand against the domination of corporate politics that the police were forced to call for back up several times. Three of our people were arrested on minor charges, but we successfully caused major disruption to the event.

Picketing the Liberal Party election fundraiser at the Regent Plaza. Image: Toby Dite

BUILDING UP POLITICAL PRESSURE 91

Premier Napthine himself was forced to sneak into the venue via a fire escape. Most importantly, it sent a message to the big end of town that this government was not in control and would struggle to build the East-West toll road even if re-elected.

SCRAP THE EAST-WEST TUNNEL!

Recent polls show that less than a quarter of Victorians support the $8 billion East-West tunnel. A recent Herald Sun poll showed just 15% support! People are seeing through the government propaganda. We know that Victoria desperately needs investment in public transport, not another toll road.

Even the government's own reports predict the East-West toll road would not reduce congestion, yet it would consume the bulk of Victoria's transport funding for decades to come. While the project will create some jobs, they would only be temporary.

Public transport projects create more long term and sustainable jobs than roads projects do. Expansion of public transport would also take more cars off the road, reducing traffic for those who need to drive. Public transport is also a key factor in reducing carbon emissions.

Despite the unpopularity of the East West tunnel the Napthine government is trying to undemocratically rush the project through before the November State election. The government does not have a mandate to do this, especially considering they said they would prioritise public transport, not the East West Link, in the lead up to the last election.

Labor has criticised the East West tunnel, but has said a Labor government would honour any contracts signed – meaning they plan for it to go ahead.

Only a strong community campaign can stop this monstrosity from going ahead. Our community picket has put a lot of pressure on Napthine. Now, in the lead up to the November 29 Victorian Election we need to demand all opposition parties and candidates commit to these three demands:

Did you know?

- One train = 800 cars off the road. More trains means reducing congestion for those who need to drive.
- The East-West Link is likely to *increase* traffic on already busy roads such as Hoddle Street and Chandler Highway
- There are thousands more skilled, long term and sustainable jobs in public transport than road projects
- The East West Link will be underwritten by taxpayers. If it is not profitable it will be us who compensates the private investors!

① SCRAP THE EAST-WEST TUNNEL — An $8 billion dollar disaster, the East-West tunnel will not help reduce Melbourne's traffic congestion problems. The government's own expert panel advised against making the East West Link as a priority project!

② RIP UP THE CONTRACTS — The Napthine Government has no mandate to build the East West tunnel. The Liberal's went into the last election saying public transport was their priority, not the East West tunnel! Breaking of contracts has been done before. It can be done again!

③ INVEST IN PUBLIC TRANSPORT — Victoria needs serious investment to bring our public transport system up to world standards. Continuing to prioritise building toll roads instead of public transport will have huge social, environmental and financial ramifications for decades to come.

A leaflet we circulated in the lead up to the election. Image: Mel Gregson

92 BEATING THE BIG END OF TOWN

Illustration by Michelle Baginski. Poster by Mel Gregson

SCRAP THE EAST-WEST TUNNEL
RIP UP THE CONTRACTS
INVEST IN PUBLIC TRANSPORT

Organised by community groups against the east-west tunnel

WE WANT TRAINS NOT tolls!

Rally: June 28

meet at 1pm
@ THE STATE LIBRARY OF VICTORIA

For more info txt 'trains not tolls' to 0432447036
or visit www.facebook.com/EastWestTunnelPledge

CHAPTER 7
THE ELECTION AND CAMPAIGN VICTORY

A few days after we ruined the Liberal Party election fundraiser, former Liberal MP Geoff Shaw came out opposing the East-West Link. Shaw, who held the balance of power in the Victorian House of Representatives, was mired in a corruption scandal and was temporarily suspended from parliament. He was looking for ways to increase his election chances and realised there was very little support for the project in his outer suburban seat of Frankston. We knew this from the discussions we had in this area during our caravan tour.

While Shaw was an unashamed opportunist this move meant that, formally at least, a majority in the state parliament now claimed to be opposed to the project. Shaw indicated that he would support legislation to stop the government signing the East-West toll road contracts before the 2014 state election. Despite now having the numbers to stop the signing of the contracts Labor refused to table a bill, cementing our distrust of their stated opposition to the project.

This gave us more reason to continue targeting inner-city Labor MPs by picketing their offices. We also continued to picket the offices of construction giant Lend Lease. On September 10, not long after we concluded a picket of the Lend Lease office in Melbourne's Docklands, Labor announced a renewed position relating to the East-West toll road.

Throughout the campaign Labor had changed its position from support, to agnosticism, to "fake" opposition. Labor now recognised that our campaign was having success in exposing the fact that if elected, a Labor government planned to go ahead and build the East-West toll road. While falling short of fully submitting to our demand to "rip up the contracts", Labor announced that if it won the November 29 election, the new Labor government would not defend the Supreme Court challenge being waged by Moreland and Yarra Councils.

In the weeks prior to this announcement Labor had conducted a phone poll asking whether voters supported the idea of ripping up any East-West toll road contracts signed prior to the election. Our campaign had put this issue on the political agenda. While Labor remained reluctant to unsettle its corporate backers, it needed to find a way to direct the growing opposition to the project into votes at the election.

Forever avoiding the taking of responsibility for its policies, Labor hoped instead to use a legal ruling to invalidate the contracts. This, Labor politicians felt, would let them off the hook as they could claim it was a decision of the court. Worried that even this soft approach might upset some in the oil and road lobby, Labor leader Daniel Andrews was nervous and sweating profusely when he made the announcement to the media.

This refined fence-sitting reflected Labor's conflicting interests. On the one hand the East-West toll road was increasingly unpopular, so coming out against it could win votes. It was a key issue with which Labor could differentiate itself from an unpopular Liberal government. On the other hand, Labor needed to ensure it was satisfying the wishes of its financial backers in the oil, road and construction lobby.

In walking this tightrope, alongside the announcement about the Supreme Court case came commitments to a number of other road projects worth billions of dollars and very profitable to big business. These included the West Gate Distributor and the removal of fifty

Picket outside the office of Labor Party state MP Jennifer Kanis. Photo Kathleen Galea

level crossings. Daniel Andrews also announced a plan to privatise the Port of Melbourne to pay for these new road projects.

Though Labor's renewed position on the East-West toll road was still short of genuine opposition, each new announcement painted them further in a corner.

LIBERALS STICK TO THEIR GUNS

For their part the Liberals had no real option but to go into the election sticking to their guns. Anything else would have made them appear weak and wavering. They had placed all their eggs in the East-West toll road basket, and while this basket was full of holes, it was they only one they had.

In a sign that the government felt it could not convince Victorians of the merits of the East-West toll road, it turned instead to blackmail. The Liberals claimed that if the project was cancelled it would impact poorly on business confidence and that nobody would want to invest in the State of Victoria. Dramatising the issue beyond belief, Planning Minister Matthew Guy claimed that not honouring the East-West toll road contracts presented a sovereign risk and Victoria's premier credit rating would be put in danger!

In late September there were also a few days of drama in the courts. The case being brought by picketer Tony Murphy was being heard. Tony's legal team, led by Ron Merkel QC, were attempting to

96   BEATING THE BIG END OF TOWN

get an injunction to stop the government from signing the contracts. Ultimately the court decided against issuing an injunction, although the case did help further delay the process.

While the government was eventually able to sign the contracts in late September, it was not a stamp of authority and confidence in the project that it had hoped for. The business case was still kept secret, the consultation process was visibly a sham and a protester almost derailed the contract signing through the courts. This all fed into the uncertainty we had created around the project.

News broke in the following days about how close everything was coming to falling apart. Even before the court was due to make a decision about an injunction, the successful bidders were getting cold feet. Lend Lease, who were later awarded the contract, threatened to pull out of the whole thing. Had it done so, the government would have been sent back to square one as the other major bidder had already pulled out.

The media reported that an emergency cabinet meeting had taken place whereby the government agreed on some extraordinary terms. In order to steel up confidence in the project, Lend Lease were issued with a special "side letter". The side letter would make the consortium eligible for hundreds of millions of dollars in compensation if the

Occuping Treasury Place during the 'Corporate Corruption Tour'. Image: Sue Jackson

Moreland and Yarra Council case was successful in stopping the project.

This was an unashamed gift to big business delivered in an act of desperation. It demonstrated total contempt for Victorian taxpayers. In its attempt to stay on course the government was digging a deeper hole.

The day after the contracts were signed we organised an action in the Melbourne CBD dubbed the "Corporate Corruption Tour". We protested outside the offices of some of the companies that made up the winning consortium, as well as Liberal Party HQ. We then occupied the foyer of the Department of Transport and finished by picketing Treasury Place, where the Premier's office is located. These actions were aimed at highlighting who was behind the East-West toll road and demonstrating that they would not proceed without constant disruption.

GREENS IN THE BACKGROUND

It was notable that during this time when criticism was beginning to be heaped on the Napthine government and its dud East-West toll road, that neither Labor or the Greens played a major role in the political debate. Clearly Labor thought it best to not highlight any further the conflicting interests bound up in their position. But the Greens could have played more of a role exposing the East-West toll road for the scam that it was.

While the Greens were consistently opposed to the East-West Link they were never the driving force in the community campaign. A handful of Greens rank-and-file members participated in the community pickets, and a few Green MPs dropped in a couple of times. A few rallies were organised by the Greens on the western side of where the toll road would be built, and some speeches were made in parliament.

98   BEATING THE BIG END OF TOWN

The Greens preferred to direct their energy and resources towards their election work, rather than community organising in a direct action campaign. From the outset they were focused on the November 2014 state election. However, the election only became a major factor in the campaign because our community campaign had forced Labor into a corner. If we had have waited until a few months before the election to organise against the project we would have failed. Originally the government had planned to start construction of the East-West toll road prior to the election. This schedule was rendered impossible by our direct action campaign.

The main strategy outlined by the Greens was based on them winning more seats in the Victorian Parliament. They argued that if their MPs had the balance of power they would be able to get the project cancelled. However, a genuine concern was whether or not they would actually exercise their power in such a scenario.

The Greens had held the effective balance of power in both houses of the federal parliament during the last Labor government. Many deeply unpopular policies were pursued by this government, yet the Greens were not able to stop them from being implemented. In Tasmania the Greens had formed a coalition with Labor and helped implement cuts and privatisations.

Unlike the Greens of the 1980s that led environmental campaigns like those against the Franklin Dam, today's Greens are single-mindedly focused on elections. This focus has led them to alienating their activist roots and becoming incorporated into the mainstream political establishment. Many of their members actually opposed our community pickets, arguing that we should leave politics in the hands of the politicians. This sentiment is a reflection of where the Greens focus their time.

On many occasions our campaign had to drag politicians into opposing the East-West toll road and supporting the campaign to stop it. Unfortunately, though not surprisingly, this was sometimes as true

THE ELECTION AND CAMPAIGN VICTORY 99

with the Greens as it was with Labor.

BEHIND THE SCENES

Behind the scenes some elected Greens waivered on important aspects of the campaign. They initially opposed Yarra Council taking legal action against the project. They also initially opposed Yarra Council setting aside money to fund a campaign in support of public transport. In 2011 the Socialist Party put forward a proposal to set aside $100,000 for a pro-public transport campaign. The Labor, Green and Independent majority on the Council all initially laughed at the proposal and refused the request.

It was only after we had organised wide support for the idea amongst the local community and environment groups that they felt pressured to support it. This was the proposal that led to Yarra Council's "Trains Not Toll Roads" campaign, an early thorn in the side of the Liberal government.

In the midst of our community picket, two of the three Greens on Yarra Council supported a motion to tow away our campaign caravan. It was an important piece of campaign infrastructure that functioned simultaneously as a blockade and as our campaign HQ. Because a local business owner had complained about the caravan blocking his view of Brunswick Street, the Greens and Labor councillors planned to remove it. It was only after this plan was leaked that they realised the decision would reflect badly on them and they retreated.

While there are many points of disagreement between the Greens and socialists in relation to policy and action, a crucial difference is how they operate in elected positions. For socialists, these positions should be used to give a voice to working class people and expose the corporate interests behind the major parties. By using these positions to give a platform to communities in struggle we can strengthen the movements that have the potential to effect real change. For the

100 BEATING THE BIG END OF TOWN

Greens, they use these positions to try and clean up the edges of society's problems and to tweak government policy. In doing so, the Greens always vote for government budgets, effectively voting to fund the policies and programs they say they oppose like the offshore processing of refugees, cuts to education and health funding, and the prioritising of roads over public transport.

The Greens claim that it would be irresponsible for them to block supply to a government and its budget. However, by helping maintain the status quo they are contributing to the major parties' pro-business agenda. For them, stability in the parliament is more important than stopping anti-worker and anti-environment policies from being enacted. It is this fundamental difference between Greens and socialists that means we approach elections very differently.

SOCIALIST ATTITUDE TO ELECTIONS

Throughout the campaign the Socialist Party used the elections to highlight the issues surrounding the East-West Link. We stood in the area where the East-West toll road would begin at both the 2013 federal election and at the 2014 state election.

In both cases a key focus of our campaigns was opposition to

Putting pressure on Labor in the lead up to the Victorian state election. Image: Chris Starr

THE ELECTION AND CAMPAIGN VICTORY 101

the East-West Link. At election time people are forced to become spectators in a dog and pony show and pick a side, even when none of the candidates on offer represent their interests. Instead of simply joining the parade, we attempted to use our candidacy to reroute the whole thing, instead focusing the debate on the East-West toll road and our alternatives.

We launched our 2014 state election campaign well before all the other parties and used it as another means to pressure Labor who held the seat of Richmond. Our first poster read "Labor say they are against the East-West tunnel... But why won't they rip up the contracts?" These posters were plastered across the electorate and we letterboxed tens of thousands of leaflets explaining the issue. The process of pressuring Labor to commit to stronger opposition to the East-West toll road actually lost us votes, but it won us the much more important victory against the road.

Elections are just one forum for politics among many. Throughout history social change has not begun within the walls of parliaments. It is always driven by the shifting expectations and active mobilisations of ordinary people - those of us who come to crash the party.

Acknowledging this, we use election campaigns, and elected positions when we win them, as platforms for the interests of ordinary people and as a megaphone for the campaigns and struggles on the ground. This approach wins us far more than would otherwise be within our reach.

Despite having no MPs in the parliament and only one councillor in the City of Yarra, the Socialist Party's political intervention helped force the issue of the East-West Link to the top of the political agenda. The polarised situation we helped to create was even recognised by Prime Minister Tony Abbott when he described the state election as a referendum on the East-West Link - a proclamation he must have later regretted!

Abbott weighed in because the campaign threatened not only

the Victorian Liberal government, but also threatened the logic of his own government. Upon winning the election in 2013 Abbott said in his first speech as Prime Minister: "we'll build the roads of the 21st century because I hope to be an infrastructure prime minister who puts bulldozers on the ground and cranes into our skies."

The East-West toll road was the largest of these projects and he was angered that it was in danger. He threatened to withdraw the $3 billion in federal funding for the road if a new Labor government did not go ahead with it. Abbott's signature heavy-handed approach ended up damaging the Liberals during the election campaign. Abbott and the federal Liberal Party were deeply unpopular at the time, especially in the minds of Victorians.

Abbott chiming in on the East-West Link was a gift. Not only did it help further polarise the situation, it helped to back Labor even further into a corner. If Labor were to win the election and build the East-West toll road it would appear as though the Labor Party was too scared to stand up to Tony Abbott. This is not the impression a new government wants to give.

We did everything we could to keep the issue of public transport front and centre all the way up to election day. Our aim was to hammer the Liberals and push Labor further into opposing the East-West toll road. We organised another citywide rally in the fortnight before election day to keep the pressure on.

By this point a number of media outlets had taken up our question, asking Labor leader Daniel Andrews whether or not his government would be willing to "rip up the contracts" if elected. In response he said "There is nothing to walk away from, be very clear about this, the contracts are not worth the paper they're written on... This is not a legally binding contract." He also claimed that, therefore "[t]here will be no compensation paid". His hope was that by not defending the Moreland and Yarra Council Supreme Court case the contracts would be ruled invalid and that compensation would not be

THE ELECTION AND CAMPAIGN VICTORY 103

an issue.

In the week of the election we also organised a rally on Bendigo Street in Collingwood. This focused on the homes that had been compulsorily acquired by the government and slated for demolition. We demanded that Labor commit to returning these homes to their owners immediately upon winning the election. This protest was well-attended and received good media coverage. Our aim was to do all we could to make it politically impossible for Labor to go back on its word.

The election on November 29, 2014 saw the Liberals decisively defeated. Labor won 47 of the 88 seats in the lower house where government is formed. It was well understood that that the East-West Link was one of the main reasons Victorians kicked the government out of office. Not only were we on the doorstep of victory against the East-West toll road but we had brought down a government in the process!

Holding Labor to account. Image: Mel Gregson

Poster by Michelle Baginski.

THE 2014 TRANSPORT ELECTION: WE DEMAND OUR SAY!

Organised by a coalition of public transport community groups.

SCRAP THE EAST-WEST LINK, RIP UP THE CONTRACTS & INVEST IN PUBLIC TRANSPORT

RALLY SATURDAY 15 NOVEMBER

1 PM State Library of Victoria

FOR MORE INFO TEXT 'TRAINS NOT TOLLS' TO 0432 447 036 OR VISIT ycat.org.au

CHAPTER 8
PLANNING FOR PEOPLE NOT PROFITS

Our success in making the East-West toll road a key election issue prompted many to view the election as a "referendum" on the project. With the government defeated, we had won this de facto referendum. However, this did not automatically guarantee the scrapping of the East-West toll road.

Throughout the entire campaign Labor had positioned itself to appear opposed to the project yet put forward arguments as to why it would be irresponsible to pull out. The first few days and weeks following the election would give us an indication of whether the new Labor government believed it could backtrack on its commitment to oppose the toll road.

Frustrated by the outcome of the election Abbott continued to demand that the new Labor Premier, Daniel Andrews, reverse his position and proceed with the project. This actually had the opposite effect of steeling Andrews against the project, as conceding to a deeply unpopular Liberal Prime Minister in his first days in office would have been political suicide.

In effect, Abbott's continued pestering hindered those supporting the East-West toll road as it made it harder for Labor to backslide without looking weak. Within a week of the election it was clear that Labor was well and truly in a corner and would not be able to proceed with the project, at least in the short term.

As the final nail in the coffin of the East-West toll road came

106   BEATING THE BIG END OF TOWN

through the outcome of an election, there was a danger of people perceiving that it was *only* the election, and not the community campaign, that led to this victory. The truth was that we had dragged Labor kicking and screaming every step of the way.

In order to register this as a community victory we organised a street party at our campaign HQ on December 13, 2014. Around 200 came out at short notice to celebrate the death of the project and listen to activists give an oral history of the long and vibrant campaign against it. What was emphasised on this day was that it was the direct action and the bold approach of the campaign that was crucial to achieving this victory.

Prior to the election Labor had promised to release the business case and the contracts relating to the toll road. The business case was released on December 15 and it confirmed everything we had warned of and more. In the new government's own words, the project was not financially viable. No wonder the business case had been kept under lock and key!

One estimate said that it would return only 45 cents for every dollar invested. It was only made attractive to private investors via promises of taxpayer subsidies to the tune of $340 million a year for at least 25 years. The government also looked at plans to toll other

Community victory street party on Westgarth Street, Fitzroy. Image: Chris Starr

roads in order to help cover the costs. Even at this rate it would have taken at least 56 years to repay the costs of building a road that few commuters would use. This would have cemented Melbourne's designation as a car-dependent city.

The business case and the details of the public-private partnership arrangement highlighted the obscene nature of neoliberal capitalism. As far as the major parties are concerned their job is to facilitate the profits of big business no matter what the cost to ordinary people, our communities and the environment. Both parties consistently introduce counter-reforms reducing welfare and access to basic social services for working class people while building a corporate welfare state. It is this process that has contributed to the growing gap between rich and poor that we see today.

Despite claiming the contracts were invalid and that no compensation would be paid the new Labor government manoeuvred to postpone the Moreland and Yarra Supreme Court case while it negotiated with the Lend Lease consortium. This indicated that some type of payout was on the cards. While some in the consortium were happy to walk away with a token payment others wanted the side letter enforced and a compensation payout of up to $1 billion.

After months of discussions the new Labor government finally entered into an in-principle agreement with the Lend Lease consortium in April 2015. The toll road would be officially cancelled and compensation as such would not be paid, although around $339 million of state funds that had been handed over to the consortium by the previous Liberal government would not be recovered. These funds, they claim, were spent by the consortium on the bidding process and on preliminary works.

While the loss of millions of dollars of taxpayers' money for nothing in return is outrageous, the loss is roughly equivalent to the corporate subsidy the state would have paid to the consortium every year for the life of the contract.

The treachery of the Liberals signing both the East-West toll road contracts and the side letter moments before being kicked out of office will hopefully be long remembered. However, Labor is equally to blame.

Labor sat on the fence up until the eleventh hour. This gave the consortium the impression that a Labor government would follow through with the project if it were locked in by the previous government. The "ransom note" that was the side letter gave the consortium the bargaining chip they felt they needed to pull Labor into line.

Had Labor committed to staunch opposition to the project the moment our community began organising the outcome could have been very different. If Andrews had strongly stated early on that a government under his leadership would never build the East-West toll road, the consortium would likely not have taken the risk. The risks were already significant enough for one of the consortia bidding for the project to pull out. A clear position from Labor could have forced the Lend Lease consortium to pull out as well.

At the end of the day, Labor is just as willing to represent the interests of big business as the Liberals. Labor would have happily gone along with the East-West toll road had the community opposition not been so vocal, forceful and effective. Waiting until the last moment to decide whether or not to oppose the project was not an oversight, but was the conscious political strategy of a party looking out for the interests of big business.

BLOW TO THE POLITICIANS' BIG BUSINESS AGENDA

The inability of either major party to push forward with the East-West toll road was a setback to the economic agenda being pushed by big business. Our community campaign demonstrated how the pro-big business agenda being carried out by the major parties can be pushed back. Our campaign gave a glimpse of the type of political strategy and community organising necessary to reverse the trend towards increasing corporate welfare and growing wealth inequality.

The defeat of the East-West toll road was a huge blow to the Liberals. Those minsters and MPs who at the time viewed themselves as all-powerful are now sitting on the opposition benches. Denis Napthine is no longer the leader of the Liberal Party in Victoria and former Transport Minister Terry Mulder, who was a political architect of the project, has been demoted to the backbench.

Labor is now under pressure from the public to deliver the goods on public transport after decades of neglect. However, the new government will mainly be looking to appease big business by carrying out a pro-roads program under another guise (and perhaps even parts of the East-West toll road project under another name).

In the meantime, those who stood their ground in the face of eviction from their homes have won the right to stay. The communities of Melbourne's inner-north have been defended and the beautiful Royal Park has been saved from ruin. This victory has also opened up the possibility of rerouting Victoria's transport future, kicking off a debate about the desperate need for investment in public transport. While this needs to be reinforced by further community organising, the space to do so has now opened up.

The campaign against the East-West toll road was a much-needed example of successful community organising and people power. Victories like this one show that people do not have to put up with whatever the political establishment dishes out to them. We can fight back and we can win. This campaign helped demonstrate that political outcomes are determined by those who struggle. Only by mobilising people into action can you begin to impact on those in power. In this case the community pickets and other bold forms of direct action took the issue out of the realm of abstract debate and decision-making behind closed doors and placed it front and centre in the public sphere.

As proud as we are of what we have achieved, it is a win that is only temporary. It is most likely that at some stage in the future another pro-big business government will rehash a proposal for an East-West toll road at the behest of their financial backers. Within a profit driven system all reforms that favour people over profit are limited.

The only way to put an end to this constant struggle between the drive for profits and community need is to change the system itself. This means challenging capitalism as the model upon which society is organised. As socialists our ultimate goal is to reshape society so that production is democratically organised to meet the needs of people and the planet, not line the pockets of wealthy individuals.

Only a system that is based on the public ownership of big industry, genuine democratic control and management at all levels of society, and sustainable, long-term planning, can achieve this.

By 2016 the world's wealthiest 1% will have passed the threshold of owning and controlling more wealth than the other 99% combined. In Australia, after years of economic boom our living standards have begun to decline. As the economic situation worsens big business and their collaborators in government will push for ordinary people to shoulder even more of the burden. This means decreasing wages and more insecure work. It means further cuts to social services and more public assets sold off to the private sector. It also means more projects like the East-West toll road will be proposed to maximise private profit at taxpayers' expense.

It doesn't have to be this way. There is more than enough wealth and resources to ensure an improved standard of living for all if it is distributed in an equal and democratic way. The obstacles to this are not technical. They are political. With the right ideas and approach the rule of big business can be broken.

REPRESENTATION FOR THE 99%

What this dispute has shown is that the major parties and the capitalists are not all-powerful. In reality their biggest strength is the weakness of working class political representation. While big business has two parties to choose from ordinary people have no mass party to call their own. The task ahead is to build a new political vehicle, one that unashamedly represents the interests of the 99%.

If progressive community groups, fighting trade unions, environment groups and the existing left organisations came together to form a new political vehicle around a program of opposing cuts, privatisations and the domination of big business it would have the potential to rally thousands of people behind progressive campaigns. Victories like those achieved against the East-West toll road could be replicated all over the country, and on a much larger scale. What the Socialist Party achieved by mobilising people into action against the East-West toll road is just a glimpse of what could be achieved by a new workers' party that had the backing of unions and other progressive forces.

We hope that the campaign against the East-West toll road has demonstrated what can happen when people stand up and fight back against the big end of town. As we celebrate the success of this inspiring community campaign we continue to fight for a world where these struggles are no longer necessary – a world where the needs of people and the environment are prioritised above all else.

Poster by Michelle Baginski.

TIMELINE

1969 – Melbourne Transport Plan released by the Bolte Liberal government. Includes plans for the F-19 Freeway (now renamed the Eastern Freeway)

1970 – Construction of F-19 Freeway begins amidst much controversy

1971 – Residents begin to organise and protest against the F-19 Freeway project

October 1977 – Height of protests against the F-19 project including two months of pickets and barricades on Alexandra Parade

December 1977 – Eastern Freeway opens to traffic after police remove protesters and barricades from Alexandra Parade

June 1994 – Coalition of environment and community groups come together to campaign against the widening of Alexandra Parade

May 1999 – Kennett Liberal government introduces idea of a link between the Eastern and Tullamarine Freeway

September 1999 – Kennett loses power and the project idea is not taken up by the Bracks Labor minority government

April 2008 – Eddington Report proposing the East-West Link released by the Brumby Labor government

June 2008 – Yarra Campaign Against the Tunnel set up at a meeting initiated by the Socialist Party at Fitzroy Town Hall

July 2008 – 200 people attend rally at Smith Reserve in Fitzroy organised by Yarra Campaign Against the Tunnel opposing plans for an East-West toll road

December 2008 – Brumby commits to building western section of the East-West Link and postpones plans for the tunnel at the eastern end

November 2010 – Brumby Labor government loses power and the new Baillieu Liberal government shelves all of Labor's transport plans

April 2011 – Socialist Party propose $100,000 be set aside in Yarra City Council budget for a pro-public transport campaign

May 2013 – New Liberal Premier Denis Napthine puts East-West Link project back on agenda and commits to funding it in the 2013-14 budget

June 2013 – Yarra Council formally launch "Trains Not Toll Roads" pro-public transport campaign

20 July 2013 – 200 people attend meeting at the North Yarra Community Health Centre called by Socialist Party Councillor Stephen Jolly

30 July 2013 – Labor modify its message on East-West Link saying they are now opposed but will honour any contracts signed

31 August 2013 – 300 attend "Say No to the Tunnel" rally organised by the Socialist Party at Smith Reserve Fitzroy

22 September 2013 – Public meeting called by Socialist Party to organise first picket against East-West Link test drilling

24 September 2013 – First day of community picketing against East-West Link test drilling on corner of Alexandra Parade East & Rutland Street in Clifton Hill

2 October 2013 – Picket line caravan/campaign HQ set up over a proposed drill site on the corner of Westgarth and Brunswick Streets in Fitzroy

9 October 2013 – After three weeks of community pickets government announces an end to test drilling

13 October 2013 – 500 attend "Community Rally Against the Tunnel" at the campaign HQ on Westgarth Street Fitzroy

15 October 2013 – Tunnel Picket group begins series of actions at offices of project bidders John Holland (subsidiary of Leighton) and Lend Lease

20 November 2013 – Tunnel Picket groups targets Linking Melbourne Authority offices in Glen Waverley

10 December 2013 – State government announces new "move-on" laws aimed at pickets and a police task force to oversee East-West related protests

15 December 2013 – 500 attend "Better Public Transport" Xmas rally organised by Tunnel Picket group at Smith Reserve in Fitzroy

16 December 2013 – Government restarts test drilling amidst massive police operation. Protesters respond by blocking roads at Brunswick Street and Alexandra Parade Fitzroy

17 December 2013 – Around 150 people attend community picket on Westgarth Street in response to government restarting test drilling

18 December 2013 – Huge battle takes place on Westgarth Street with picketers pulling down fences and scaling drill rigs

20 December 2013 – Government suspends test drilling for summer break

8 January 2014 – Government announces another restart to test drilling saying that fourteen more drill sites will be required

18 February 2014 – 3,000 attend Trades Hall organised rally against the new "move-on" laws

5 March 2014 – After several weeks of daily pickets government gives up on test drilling for a third time

12 March 2014 – "Move-on" laws passed through Victorian parliament. Four people arrested for protesting in the chamber

18 March 2014 – Protesters begin targeting water testing works on Alexandra Parade

21 March 2014 – Tunnel Picket group protests against Premier Denis Napthine on Smith Street, Fitzroy. Police car carrying Premier drives through picket and breaks a protesters foot

26 March 2014 – First five people face the Magistrates Court on minor charges relating to the community pickets

30 March 2014 – 2,000 people attend rally on Sydney Road Brunswick organised by Moreland Campaign Against the Tunnel

5 April 2014 – Caravan tour launched promoting June 28 Rally4PT. Tour visits numerous suburban and regional locations over three month period

22 April 2014 – Tony Murphy launches Supreme Court challenge to the project

4 May 2014 – Rally organised by Moreland Campaign Against the Tunnel highlighting impacts project would have on the Melbourne Zoo

28 June 2014 – 3,000 attend Rally4PT in Melbourne CBD. Protesters occupy Flinders and Swanston Street intersection

30 June 2014 – Government formally approves plans for the project

18 July 2014 – Moreland Council agrees to launch action against the project in the Supreme Court

19 July 2014 – Tunnel Picket group pushes for supporters to lobby Yarra Councillors demanding they join Moreland Council's Supreme Court challenge

21 July 2014 – Yarra Council agree to join Moreland Council's Supreme Court challenge to the project

1 August 2014 – Tunnel Picket group begins targeting the offices of inner-city Labor MPs demanding they pledge to rip up any contracts signed starting with Richard Wynne's office in Collingwood

22 August 2014 – Tunnel Picket group targets Labor MP Jane Garret's office in Brunswick

28 August 2014 – Tunnel Picket group targets Liberal Party $10,000 a head fundraiser at Regent Plaza Ballroom

30 August 2014 – Balance of power MP Geoff Shaw comes out against the East-West Link meaning majority of parliament now formally opposed

5 September 2014 – Tunnel Picket group targets Labor MP Jennifer Kanis' office in North Melbourne

10 September 2014 – Tunnel Picket group targets Lend Lease HQ. Labor change position saying they will not defend Moreland/Yarra Supreme Court case

1 October 2014 – Tunnel Picket group organises "Corporate Corruption Tour" to protest government signing contracts with the Lend Lease consortium

15 November 2014 – 1,500 attend second major Rally4PT in Melbourne CBD

25 November 2014 – Tunnel Picket group protest on Bendigo Street demanding home acquisition process be reversed if Labor win election

29 November 2014 – Liberals lose power at Victorian state election. New Labor government says it will not proceed with the East-West Link

13 December 2014 – 200 attend victory party held on corner of Westgarth & Brunswick Streets Fitzroy

15 December, 2014 – Business case released vindicating all the arguments made by opponents of the project

January 2015 – Linking Melbourne Authority disbanded

April 2015 – East-West toll road dispute finally concluded with the Andrews Labor government cancelling the project and coming to an arrangement with the Lend Lease led consortium

NO TUNNEL NO WAY
A SONG WRITTEN BY LAURA MACFARLANE

It's our city it's our town
Who has the right to tear it down
This tunnel makes no sense
Built for greed and moneys end
See the people hand in hand
Come together take a stand
This ain't no missing link
So what do you say what do you think

No tunnel no way
Let the people have their say
No tunnel no way
Were gonna fight it all the way.
No tunnel no way
Give us a train not another tollway
No tunnel no way
We're gonna fight it all the way.

It's his home and his home is his castle
You wanna tear it down for this total disaster
This tunnel makes no sense
Built for greed and moneys end
We can win this if we come together
Sister brother brother sister
This ain't no missing link
So what do you say what do you think

No tunnel no way
Let the people have their say
No tunnel no way
Were gonna fight it all the way.
No tunnel no way

Give us a train not another tollway
No tunnel no way
We're gonna fight it all the way.
No tunnel no way
Let the people have their say
No tunnel no way
Give us a train not another tollway
No tunnel no way
Let the people have their say
No tunnel no way
Were gonna fight it all the way.

Song released 20 February 2014.

http://tunnelpicket.bandcamp.com/track/no-tunnel-no-way

Laura performing 'No Tunnel No Way' at the June 28 rally against the East-West toll road. Image: Ali Bakhtiarvanadi

ABOUT THE SOCIALIST PARTY

The Socialist Party is the Australian section of the Committee for a Workers' International (CWI). The CWI has affiliated parties and groups in more than 50 countries on all continents.

To find our more visit: www.sp.org.au & www.socialistworld.net

Socialist Party / australia.org
JOIN THE FIGHT BACK!

- (03) 9639 9111
- www.sp.org.au
- info@socialistpartyaustralia.org
- Socialist Party - Australia
- @sp_australia
- txt 'Join SP' to 0432 447 036

SUBSCRIBE TO 'THE SOCIALIST'
MONTHLY MAGAZINE OF THE SOCIALIST PARTY

'The Socialist' provides political analysis of events in Australia and internationally from a socialist perspective as well as various introductions to Marxist theory.

VISIT WWW.SP.ORG.AU TO SUBSCRIBE

Printed in Australia
AUOC02n1957130515
267575AU00013B/18/P